25 bags to knit

25 bags to knit

BEAUTIFUL BAGS IN STYLISH COLORS

Emma King

Trafalgar Square Publishing

North Pomfret, Vermont

This book is dedicated to Simon

First published in the United States of America in 2004 by
Trafalgar Square Publishing, North Pomfret, Vermont 05053

Reproduction by Mission, Hong Kong
Printed and bound by Imago Printers, Thailand

9 8 7 6 5 4

ISBN 1 57076 282 1

Library of Congress Control Number: 2004104302

EDITOR: **Emma Callery**
DESIGNER: **Justina Leitão**
PHOTOGRAPHER: **Neil Sutherland**
CHART ILLUSTRATIONS: **Anthony Duke**
PATTERN CHECKER: **Rosy Tucker**

Contents

Introduction 7

Introduction

Accessories are fun and are often used to brighten up an outfit or to make a style statement, and what better way could there be than to create your own knitted bag.

This book contains projects for all levels of knitters with simple knits through to more complicated ones, and covers a wide range of techniques including intarsia, Fair Isle, knitting with beads and sequins, and simple embroidery. Yarns and shapes have been chosen to ensure color and texture are used to full effect and, at times, the yarns are used double, triple and even quadruple.

Knitted bags are a great chance to experiment and to take risks with color, which you might not normally take if you were knitting a garment. You might want to knit Delight (see page 38), but instead of purples you'd like greens. If so, have a go at changing the colorway. If you want to work with texture, then give Marina (see page 46) a go, or if knitting with beads takes your fancy, then why not try Strawberry Gem on page 14?

The great thing about all knitted bags is that they don't take too long to knit so there's no reason why you can't make your way through all 25 of my designs! I had great fun creating them and I hope you'll have even more fun knitting them.

emma king

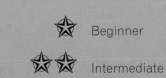

★ Beginner

★★ Intermediate

★★★ Advanced

These are a guide only. What some knitters find difficult, others find quite easy, so read the pattern before deciding whether or not to knit it.

Anytime bags

Bluebell

A medley of different yarns, including tweed and mohair, are used in stripes and Fair Isle to create a subtle bag with a very delicate use of color. The soft mohair sits alongside the robust tweed to create a fabric that is tantalizing to the touch.

SIZE
9in × 7½in (23cm × 19cm), excluding handle

MATERIALS
1 pair US 7 (4.5mm/no.7) needles

Yarn
Rowan Cotton Glacé
1¾oz (50g) balls
  sky (A)   2
  (used double throughout)

Rowan 4-ply Soft
1¾oz (50g) balls
  whisper (B)   1
  (used double throughout)

Rowan Kid Silk Haze
1oz (25g) balls
  heavenly (C)   1
  (used double throughout)

Rowan Summer Tweed
1¾oz (50g) balls
  powder (D)   1

GAUGE (TENSION)
18 sts and 25 rows to 4in (10cm) measured over pattern using US 7 (4.5mm/no.7) needles.

ABBREVIATIONS
beg	beginning
k	knit
p	purl
rem	remaining
rep	repeat
RS	right side
st st	stockinette (stocking) stitch
sts	stitches
WS	wrong side

TECHNIQUES
Fair Isle, see page 119
Sewing in ends, see page 118
Sewing up, see page 125

KNIT
Front
Using US 7 (4.5mm/no.7) needles and yarn A, cast on 45 sts.
ROW 1: k1, *p1, k1, rep from * to end.
This row forms seed (moss) stitch.
ROWS 2–14: As row 1, ending with a WS row.
Change to yarn B.
ROW 15: Knit.
Change to yarn D.
ROW 16: Purl.
ROW 17: Knit.
ROW 18: Purl.
These last 2 rows form st st stitch.
ROWS 19–20: As rows 17–18.
Change to yarn B.
ROWS 21–22: As rows 17–18.
Change to yarn C.
ROWS 23–26: As rows 17–18.
Change to yarn B.
ROW 27: Knit.
Change to yarn D.
ROW 28: Purl.
Change to yarn A.
ROWS 29–35: To be worked from chart in st st using Fair Isle (see page 119), beg with a knit (RS) row and ending with purl (WS) row.
Change to yarn B.
ROW 36: Purl.
Change to yarn D.
ROW 37: Knit.
ROW 38: Purl.
Change to yarn C.
ROW 38: Knit.
ROW 39: Purl.
Change to yarn A.
ROWS 40–47: As row 1.
ROW 48: Knit (this creates garter st ridge for turn over at top of bag).
Change to yarn B.
ROW 49: Knit.
ROW 50: Purl.
ROWS 51–54: Rep rows 49–50, ending with a WS row.
Bind (cast) off.

CHART

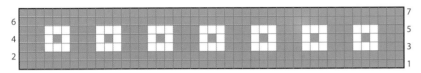

Key

■ sky (A)
□ whisper (B)

Back

Using US 7 (4.5mm/no.7) needles and yarn A, cast on 45 sts.
ROW 1: k1, *p1, k1, rep from * to end.
This row forms seed (moss) stitch.
ROWS 2–14: As row 1, ending with a WS row.
Change to yarn B.
ROW 15: Knit.
Change to yarn D.
ROW 16: Purl.
ROW 17: Knit.
ROW 18: Purl.
These last 2 rows form st st stitch.
ROWS 19–20: As rows 17–18.
Change to yarn B.
ROWS 21–22: As rows 17–18.
Change to yarn C.
ROWS 23–26: As rows 17–18.
Change to yarn B.
ROW 27: Knit.
Change to yarn D.
ROW 28: Purl.
Change to yarn A.
ROWS 29–35: As rows 17–18, then 17 again.
Change to yarn B.

ROW 36: Purl.
Change to yarn D.
ROW 37: Knit.
ROW 38: Purl.
Change to yarn C.
ROW 38: Knit.
ROW 39: Purl.
Change to yarn A.
ROWS 40–47: As row 1.
ROW 48: Knit (this creates garter st ridge for turn over at top of bag).
Change to yarn B.
ROW 49: Knit.
ROW 50: Purl.
ROWS 51–54: Rep rows 49–50, ending with a WS row.
Bind (cast) off.

Handle (make 1)

Using US 7 (4.5mm/no.7) needles and yarn A, cast on 7 sts.
ROW 1: K1, *p1, k1, rep from * to end.
Rep this row until handle measures 19¾in (50cm), ending with a WS row.
Bind (cast) off.

FINISHING

Sew in all the ends.

Using mattress stitch, join the Front and Back by working down one side, across the bottom and up the other side (see page 125). Fold down the turn over at the top of the bag along the garter st ridge and slip stitch into place using yarn B. Do this for the Front and the Back.

Slip stitch handle neatly and securely into place inside the side seams at top of bag.

Strawberry Gem

The simple Fair Isle strip at the bottom of this bag is echoed by the bead detail that runs above it. The ripe red and the delicate pink combine and complement each other to remind us of this most delicious of summer fruit. Scrumptious!

SIZE

7in × 8¼in (18cm × 21cm), excluding handle

MATERIALS

1 pair US 6 (4mm/no.8) needles

Yarn

Rowan Handknit DK Cotton
1¾oz (50g) balls

rosso (A)	2
shell (B)	1

Beads

red	approx. 34

GAUGE (TENSION)

21 sts and 27 rows to 4in (10cm) measured over stockinette (stocking) stitch using US 6 (4mm/no.8) needles.

ABBREVIATIONS

beg	beginning
k	knit
p	purl
pb	place bead: yarn forward, slip bead to front of work, sl 1 st purlwise, take yarn to back of work. Bead will now be sitting in front of slipped stitch
rem	remaining
RS	right side
sl	slip
st st	stockinette (stocking) stitch
sts	stitches
WS	wrong side

TECHNIQUES

Fair Isle, see page 119
Knitting with beads, see page 120
Sewing in ends, see page 118
Sewing up, see page 125

KNIT

Front

Using US 6 (4mm/no.8) needles and yarn A, cast on 35 sts.
ROW 1 (RS): Knit.
ROW 2 (WS): Purl.
These last 2 rows form st st.
ROWS 3–39: Work from chart 1 in st st using the Fair Isle technique described on page 119 and beg with a RS row as follows:

Work rows 3–12, then rep rows 5–12 three more times and then rows 5–7, ending with a RS row.
ROW 40: Purl.
Change to yarn B.
ROWS 41–52: Work rows 1–12 from chart 2 (overleaf), ending with a WS row.
Change to yarn A.

CHART 1

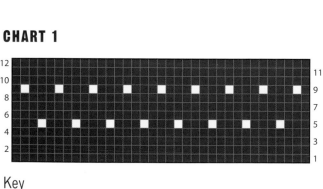

Key

☐ shell (B)

■ rosso (A)

CHART 2

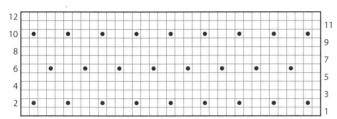

Key

⊡ pb   ☐ shell (B)

ROW 53: **Knit.**
ROW 54: **Purl.**
Change to yarn B.
ROWS 55–58: **Work rows 1–4 from chart 2, ending with a WS row.**
Change to yarn A.
ROWS 59–60: **Knit (row 60 creates a garter st ridge for turn over at top bag).**
Change to yarn B.
ROW 61: **Knit.**
ROW 62: **Purl.**
ROWS 63–68: **As rows 61–62, ending with a WS row.**
Bind (cast) off.

Back

Using US 6 (4mm/no.8) needles and yarn A, cast on 35 sts.
ROW 1: **Knit.**
ROW 2: **Purl.**
ROWS 3–40: **Rep last 2 rows, ending with a WS row.**
Change to yarn B.
ROWS 41–52: **As rows 1–2, ending with a WS row.**

Change to yarn A.
ROW 53: **Knit.**
ROW 54: **Purl.**
Change to yarn B.
ROWS 55–58: **As rows 1–2, ending with a WS row.**
Change to yarn A.
ROWS 59–60: **Knit (row 60 creates a garter st ridge for turn over at top bag).**
Change to yarn B.
ROW 61: **Knit.**
ROW 62: **Purl.**
ROWS 63–68: **As rows 61–62, ending with a WS row.**
Bind (cast) off.

Handle (make 1)

Using US 6 (4mm/no.8) needles and yarn A, cast on 5 sts.
ROW 1: **Knit.**
ROW 2: **K1, p3, k1.**
Rep last 2 rows until handle measures 11¼in (30cm), ending with a WS row.
Bind (cast) off.

FINISHING

Sew in all the ends.
 Using mattress stitch, join the Front and Back by working down one side, across the bottom and up the other side. Fold down the turn over at the top of the bag along the garter st ridge and slip stitch into place using yarn B. Do this for the Front and the Back.
 Slip stitch the handles securely in place inside the side seams at top of bag.

Fancy

Bursting with character and shape, this bag is a real show off. The spherical shape is achieved through basic shaping and it is topped with three luxurious bands of mohair and silk. This bag is a talking point and will add fun and frolics to any night out.

SIZE
12½in × 7in (32cm × 18cm), excluding handle

MATERIALS
1 pair US 6 (4mm/no.8) needles

Yarn
Rowan 4-ply Soft
1¾oz (50g) balls
    wink (A)   2
    (used double throughout)

Rowan Kid Silk Haze
1oz (25g) balls
    candy girl (B)   1
    (used double throughout)

GAUGE (TENSION)
21 sts and 30 rows to 4in (10cm) measured over pattern using US 6 (4mm/no.8) needles.

ABBREVIATIONS
beg	beginning
dec	decrease
inc	increase
k	knit
m1	make one stitch
beg	purl
rem	remaining
rep	repeat
RS	right side
st st	stockinette (stocking) stitch
sts	stitches
tog	together
WS	wrong side

TECHNIQUES
Sewing in ends, see page 118
Sewing up, see page 125

KNIT
Front and Back alike
First section
Using US 6 (4mm/no.8) needles and yarn B, cast on 173 sts.
ROW 1: K1, *k2, lift first of these 2 over second, rep from * to end.
ROW 2: (p2tog) to last st, p1. (44 sts)
Change to yarn A.
ROW 3: (RS): Knit.
ROW 4: (WS): Purl.
These two rows form st st.
ROWS 5–8: Rep rows 3 and 4 twice more, ending with a WS row.
Break off yarn and leave stitches on a holder.

Second section
Rep rows 1 and 2 of first section. You now have a second ruffle.
Slip the stitches of the first section off their holder and onto a spare needle. Place the needle of the second ruffle in front of the needle holding the first section of knitting with right sides facing. Using yarn A and a third needle, knit together the first stitch on the front needle together with the first stitch on the back needle. Continue in this way until the whole row has been completed and the second ruffle is attached.

Still using yarn A, work rows 3–8 of the first section.
Break off yarn and leave stitches on a holder.

Third section
Rep rows 1 and 2 of first section. You now have a third ruffle.
Slip the stitches of the second section off their holder and onto a spare needle. Place the needle of the third ruffle in front of the needle holding the second section of knitting with right sides facing. Using yarn A and a third needle, knit together the first stitch on the front needle together with the first stitch on the back needle. Continue in this way until the whole row has been completed and the third ruffle is attached.

Now all three ruffles have been attached, commence as follows:

Main section

Using yarn A:

ROW 1: **Purl.**

ROW 2: **Knit.**

ROWS 3: **Purl.**

ROW 4-5: **Rep last 2 rows once more, ending with a WS row.**

ROW 6: **As row 2.**

ROWS 7-8: **As rows 1 and 2.**

ROWS 9-18: **Rep row 1 ten times, ending with a WS row.**

ROW 19 (RS) (INC ROW): **k5, m1, k marked st, m1, *k6, m1, k marked st, m1, rep from * to last 5 sts, k5. (76 sts)**

ROWS 20-28: **Rep row 1 nine times, ending with a WS row.**

ROW 29 (RS) (INC ROW): **K6, m1, k marked st, m1, *k8, m1, k marked st, rep from * to last 6 sts, k6. (92 sts)**

ROWS 30-34: **Rep row 1 five times, ending with a WS row.**

ROW 35 (RS) (DEC ROW): **K5, k2tog, k marked st, k2tog, *k6, k2tog, k marked st, k2tog, rep from * to last 5 sts, k5. (76 sts)**

ROWS 36-40: **Rep row 1 five times, ending with a WS row.**

ROW 41 (RS) (DEC ROW): **K4, *k2tog, k marked st, k2tog, k4, rep from * to end. (60 sts)**

ROWS 42-46: **Rep row 1 five times,** ending with a WS row.

ROW 47 (RS) (DEC ROW): **K3, k2tog, k marked st, k2tog, *k2, k2tog, k marked st, k2tog, rep from * to last 3 sts, k3. (44 sts)**

ROWS 48-50: **Rep row 1 three times, ending with a WS row.**

ROW 51 (RS) (DEC ROW): **K2, *k2tog, k marked st, k2tog, rep from * to last 2 sts, k2. (28 sts)**

ROW 52 (WS): **As row 1.**

Bind (cast) off.

Handles (make 2)

Using US 6 (4mm/no.8) needles and yarn A, cast on 7 sts.

ROW 1: **Knit.**

ROW 2: **K1, p5, k1.**

Rep last 2 rows until handle measures 10in (25cm), ending with a WS row.

Bind (cast) off.

FINISHING

Sew in all the ends.

Using mattress stitch, join the Front and Back by working down one side, across the bottom and up the other side.

Slip stitch handles securely in place approximately ¾in (1.5cm) in from the side seams. Do this for the Front and Back.

Lemon Zest

This is a fun bag that lets the bright colors do the talking! The lime green and citrus tones are further accentuated by sharp dashes of silver lurex, garter stitch ridges and stripes. The use of seed (moss) stitch at the bottom and for the handles adds extra texture and tone to the bag.

SIZE

10¼in × 11in (26cm × 28cm), excluding handle

MATERIALS

1 pair US 9 (5.5mm/no.5) needles

Yarn

Rowan Handknit DK Cotton
1¾oz (50g) balls
    gooseberry (B)   3
    (used double throughout)
    zing (A)   1
    (used double throughout)
    celery (E)   1
    (used double throughout)

Rowan Lurex Shimmer
1¾oz (50g) balls
    pewter (C)   1
    (used triple throughout)

Rowan Kid Silk Haze
1oz (25g) balls
    jelly (D)   1
    (used quadruple throughout)

GAUGE (TENSION)

15½ sts and 21 rows to 4in (10cm) measured over stockinette (stocking) stitch using US 9 (5.5mm/no.5) needles

ABBREVIATIONS

beg	beginning
k	knit
p	purl
rem	remaining
rep	repeat
st st	stockinette (stocking) stitch
sts	stitches

TECHNIQUES

Sewing in ends, see page 118
Sewing up, see page 125

KNIT

Front

Using US 9 (5.5mm/no.5) needles cast on 45 sts using B.

ROW 1: Using yarn B, *k1, p1, rep from * to last st, k1 (this sets seed (moss) st).

ROWS 2–14: Using yarn B, seed (moss) st, as set by row 1.

Rows 15–19 are to be worked in st st, beg with a k row.

ROWS 15–17: Using yarn E.

ROW 18: Using yarn A.

ROW 19: Using yarn D.

Rows 20–23 are to be worked in garter st, k every row.

ROW 20: Using yarn E.

ROW 21: Using yarn A.

ROW 22: Using yarn C.

ROW 23: Using yarn E.

ROW 24: Purl using yarn E.

Rows 25–27 are to be worked in seed (moss) st, as set by row 1.

ROWS 25–26: Using yarn B.

TIP

When binding (casting) off and then casting on again on the next row to make the handle, it is like making a very big buttonhole. To avoid the annoying loop that you can get in the corner of the "buttonhole," on row 52 (Front) when you have to cast on 19 sts, in between the 18th and 19th cast-on sts, bring the yarn to the front so it is trapped between the two.

ROW 27: **Using yarn E.**
Rows 28–33 are to be worked in st st, beg with a p row.
ROWS 28–31: **Using yarn E.**
ROW 32: **Using yarn A.**
ROW 33: **Using yarn D.**
Rows 34–37 are to be worked in garter st, k every row.
ROW 34: **Using yarn E.**
ROW 35: **Using yarn A.**
ROW 36: **Using yarn C.**
ROW 37: **Using yarn E.**
Rows 38–46 are to be worked in st st, beg with a p row.
ROW 38: **Using yarn E.**
ROW 39: **Using yarn A.**
ROW 40: **Using yarn B.**
ROW 41: **Using yarn C.**
ROW 42: **Using yarn E.**
ROW 43: **Using yarn A.**
ROW 44: **Using yarn B.**
ROW 45: **Using yarn C.**
ROW 46: **Using yarn B.**
Rows 47–56 are to be worked in seed (moss) st, as set by row 1.
ROWS 47–50: **Using yarn B.**
ROW 51: **Still using yarn B, work 13 sts, bind (cast) off center 19 sts, work to end.**
ROW 52: **Still using yarn B, work 13 sts, turn, cast on center 19 sts (see Tip), turn, work to end.**
ROWS 53–56: **Using yarn B.**
Bind (cast) off.

Back

Using US 9 (5.5mm/no.5) needles and yarn B, cast on 45 sts.
ROW 1: **Using yarn B, *k1, p1, rep from * to last st, k1 (this sets seed (moss) st).**

ROWS 2–14: **Using yarn B, seed (moss) st, as set by row 1.**
Rows 15–44 are to be worked in st st, beg with a k row.
ROWS 15–23: **Using yarn E.**
ROW 24: **Using yarn C.**
ROW 25: **Using yarn D.**
ROWS 26–33: **Using yarn B.**
ROW 34: **Using yarn C.**
ROW 35: **Using yarn D.**
ROWS 36–43: **Using yarn A.**
ROW 44: **Using yarn B.**

Rows 45–54 are to worked in seed (moss) st, as set by row 1.
ROWS 45–48: **Using yarn B.**
ROW 49: **Still using yarn B, work 13 sts, bind (cast) off center 19 sts, work to end.**
ROW 50: **Still using yarn B, work 13 sts, turn, cast on center 19 sts, (see Tip), turn, work to end.**
ROWS 51–54: **Using yarn B.**
Bind (cast) off.

FINISHING

Sew in all the ends.
   Using mattress stitch, join the Front and Back by working down one side, across the bottom and up the other side.

Blossom

The layers used to create the flower petals and leaves are the main feature of this bag and sit well on its simple stockinette (stocking) stitch and rib body. The petals might look complicated but they are, in fact, very simple to make—they just have a lot of increasing and decreasing to create their fullness.

SIZE
9in × 6¼in (23cm × 16cm), excluding handle

MATERIALS
1 pair US 8 (5mm/no.6) needles
1 pair US 3 (3.25mm/no.10) needles

Yarn
Rowan All Seasons Cotton
1¾oz (50g) balls
    black currant (A)   2*
    (*used double for sides of
    bag and handle and single
    for the flower)

Rowan Handknit DK Cotton
1¾oz (50g) balls
    sugar (B)   1*
    (*used double for sides of
    bag and handle and single
    for the flower)

Rowan Cotton Glacé
    dijon (C)   small amount

GAUGE (TENSION)
17 sts and 22 rows to 4in (10cm) measured over stockinette (stocking) stitch using US 8 (5mm/no.6) needles.

ABBREVIATIONS
alt	alternative
beg	beginning
k	knit
m1	make one
p	purl
rem	remaining
RS	right side
sl1, k1, psso	slip 1, knit 1, pass slipped stitch over
st st	stockinette (stocking) stitch
sts	stitches
tog	together
WS	wrong side
yf	yarn forward

TECHNIQUES
Sewing in ends, see page 118
Sewing up, see page 125

KNIT
Front and Back the same
Using US 8 (5mm/no.6) needles and yarn A, cast on 35 sts.
ROW 1: Knit.
ROW 2: K1 (p1, k1) to end.
ROWS 3–26: As rows 1 and 2.
Change to yarn B.
ROW 27: Knit.
ROW 28: Purl.
ROWS 29-36: As rows 27–28.
Change to yarn A.
ROW 37: Knit.
ROW 38: Knit (this creates g st ridge for turn over at top of bag).
ROW 39: Knit.
ROW 40: Purl.
Bind (cast) off.

Handle (make 1)
Using US 8 (5mm/no.6) needles and yarn A, cast on 5 sts.
ROW 1: Knit.
ROW 2: K1, p3, k1.
Rep rows 1 and 2 until handle measures 13in (33cm) or preferred length.

Flower center
Using US 3 (3.25mm/no.10) needles and yarn A, cast on 93 sts.
ROW 1: K1, *k2, lift first of these 2 over second, rep from * to end.
ROW 2: Using yarn B, p1, *p2tog, rep from * to end. (24 sts)
ROW 3: Still using yarn B, knit.
Break off yarn, thread through rem sts, pull up and secure.

Petals (make 2)

Using US 3 (3.25mm/no.10) needles and yarn A, cast on 3 sts.

ROW 1: K1, yf, k1, yf, k1. (5 sts)
ROW 2: and every alt row: Purl.
ROW 3: K2, m1, k1, m1, k2. (7 sts)
ROW 5: K3, m1, k1, m1, k3. (9 sts)
ROW 7: K4, m1, k1, m1, k4. (11 sts)
ROW 9: K3, sl1, k1, psso, k1, k2tog, k3. (9 sts)
ROW 11: K2, sl1, k1, psso, k1, k2tog, k2. (7 sts)
ROW 13: K1, sl1, k1, psso, k1, k2tog, k1. (5 sts)
ROW 15: K2tog, k1, k2tog. (3 sts)
Break off yarn, thread through 3 rem sts, pull up and secure.

1st leaf (large)

Using US 3 (3.25mm/no.10) needles and yarn C, cast on 3 sts.

ROW 1: K1, yf, k1, yf, k1. (5 sts)
ROW 2: and every alt row: Purl.
ROW 3: K2, m1, k1, m1, k2. (7 sts)
ROW 5: K3, m1, k1, m1, k3. (9 sts)
ROW 7: K4, m1, k1, m1, k4. (11 sts)
ROW 9: K5, m1, k1, m1, k5. (13 sts)
ROW 11: K4, sl1, k1, psso, k1, k2tog, k4. (11 sts)
ROW 13: K3, sl1, k1, psso, k1, k2tog, k3. (9 sts)
ROW 15: K2, sl1, k1, psso, k1, k2tog, k2. (7 sts)
ROW 17: K1, sl1, k1, psso, k1, k2tog, k1. (5 sts)
ROW 19: K2tog, k1, k2tog. (3 sts)
Break off yarn, thread through 3 rem sts, pull up and secure.

2nd leaf (small)

Using US 3 (3.25mm/no.10) needles and yarn C, cast on 3 sts.

ROW 1: K1, yf, k1, yf, k1. (5 sts)
ROW 2: and every alt row: Purl.
ROW 3: K2, m1, k1, m1, k2. (7 sts)
ROW 5: K3, m1, k1, m1, k3. (9 sts)
ROW 7: K2, sl1, k1, psso, k1, k2tog, k2. (7 sts)
ROW 9: K1, sl1, k1, psso, k1, k2tog, k1. (5 sts)
ROW 11: K2tog, k1, k2tog. (3 sts)
Break off yarn, thread through 3 rem sts, pull up and secure.

FINISHING

Sew in all ends.

Using mattress stitch, join the Front and Back by sewing down one side, across the bottom and up the other side.

Fold down the turn over at the top of the bag along the garter stitch ridge and, using yarn A, slip stitch into place. Do this for the Front and Back.

Slip stitch the handle securely in place inside the side seams at the top of the bag.

Sew the leaves and petals in place (top left of front of bag) and then attach the flower center as your finishing touch.

Black Cherry

This is a very simple bag to knit with a practical shape and handle. The design uses bold stripes and garter stitch ridges, which in turn combine with and complement the colors that I have chosen. With its even simpler back (see overleaf), this bag knits up in next to no time.

SIZE
10¼in × 11in (26 × 28cm)

MATERIALS
1 pair US 9 (5.5mm/no.5) needles

Yarn
Rowan Cotton Glacé
1¾oz (50g) balls
    hyacinth (A)   1
    (used triple throughout)

Rowan Handknit DK Cotton
1¾oz (50g) balls
    lupin (B)   2
    (used double throughout)

Rowan Lurex Shimmer
1¾oz (50g) balls
    bedazzled (C)   1
    (used triple throughout)

Rowan Kid Classic
1¾oz (50g) balls
    royal (D)   1
    (used double throughout)

GAUGE (TENSION)
15½ sts and 21 rows to 4in (10cm) measured over stockinette (stocking) stitch using US 9 (5.5mm/no.5) needles.

ABBREVIATIONS
beg	beginning
k	knit
p	purl
rem	remaining
st st	stockinette (stocking) stitch
sts	stitches

TECHNIQUES
Sewing in ends, see page 118
Sewing up, see page 125

KNIT
Front
Using US 9 (5.5mm/no.5) needles cast on 45 stitches.
The first 13 rows are to be worked in st st, beg with a k row.
ROWS 1–5: Using yarn B.
ROWS 6–7: Using yarn D.
ROW 8: Using yarn B.
ROW 9: Using yarn A.
ROW 10: Using yarn C.
ROWS 11–13: Using yarn B.
Rows 14–16 are to be worked in garter st, k every row.
ROW 14: Using yarn D.
ROW 15: Using yarn C.
ROW 16: Using yarn A.
Rows 17–29 are to be worked in st st, beg with a k row.
ROWS 17–20: Using yarn B.
ROWS 21–22: Using yarn D.

TIP

When binding (casting) off and then casting on again on the next row to make the handle, it is like making a very big buttonhole. To avoid the annoying loop that you can get in the corner of the "buttonhole," on row 49 (Front) when you have to cast on 19 sts in between the 18th and 19th cast-on sts, bring the yarn to the front so it is trapped between the two.

ROW 23: **Using yarn B.**
ROW 24: **Using yarn A.**
ROW 25: **Using yarn C.**
ROWS 26–29: **Using yarn B.**
Rows 30–32 are to be worked in garter st, k every row.
ROW 30: **Using yarn D.**
ROW 31: **Using yarn C.**
ROW 32: **Using yarn A.**
Rows 33–55 are to be worked in st st.
ROW 33: **Using yarn B.**
ROWS 34–39: **Using yarn D.**
ROWS 40–41: **Using yarn B.**
ROWS 42–44: **Using yarn A.**

ROW 45: **Using yarn C.**
ROWS 46–47: **Using yarn D.**
ROW 48: **Still using yarn D, work 13 sts, bind (cast) off center 19 sts, work to end.**
ROW 49: **Still using yarn D, work 13 sts, cast on center 19 sts (see Tip), work to end.**
ROWS 50–55: **Using yarn D.**
Bind (cast) off.

Back
Using US 9 (5.5mm/no.5) needles and yarn B, cast on 45 sts.
The entire back is worked in st st, beg with a k row.
ROWS 1–13: **Using yarn B.**
ROW 14: **Using yarn C.**
ROWS 15–26: **Using yarn A.**
ROW 27: **Using yarn C.**
ROWS 28–37: **Using yarn B.**
ROWS 38–44: **Using yarn D.**
ROW 45: **Still using yarn D, work 13 sts, bind (cast) off center 19 sts, work to end.**
ROW 46: **Still using yarn D, work 13 sts, cast on center 19 sts, work to end.**
ROWS 47–52: **Using yarn D.**
Bind (cast) off.

FINISHING
Sew in all the ends.
With right sides facing and using mattress stitch, sew down one side, across the base and up the other side.

Olive

This bag involves simple stitch work, relying on the combination of the beautiful textures of tweed and mohair to catch the eye. The subtle yellows and vibrant greens work together to accentuate the amazing range of colors found within the tweed.

SIZE

9in × 8in (23cm × 20cm), excluding handle

MATERIALS

1 pair US 6 (4mm/no.8) needles

Yarn

Rowan Yorkshire Tweed DK
1¾oz (50g) balls
    frog (A)   1

Rowan 4-ply Soft
1¾oz (50g) balls
    goblin (B)   1
    (used double throughout)

Rowan Kid Silk Haze
1oz (25g) balls
    jelly (C)   1
    (used double throughout)

GAUGE (TENSION)

21 sts and 30 rows to 4in (10cm) measured over pattern using US 6 (4mm/no.8) needles.

ABBREVIATIONS

beg	beginning
k	knit
p	purl
rem	remaining
rep	repeat
RS	right side
st st	stockinette (stocking) stitch
sts	stitches
WS	wrong side

TECHNIQUES

Sewing in ends, see page 118
Sewing up, see page 125

KNIT

Front

Using US 6 (4mm/no.8) needles and yarn A, cast on 50 sts.
ROW 1: **Knit.**
ROW 2: **K2, *p2, k2, rep from * to end.**
ROWS 3–24: **Rep rows 1 and 2 eleven more times, ending with a WS row.**
Change to yarn B.
ROW 25–28: **Rep rows 1 and 2 twice more.**
Change to yarn A.
ROW 29–30: **Rep rows 1 and 2 again, ending with a WS row.**
Change to yarn B.
ROWS 31–32: **Rep rows 1 and 2 again, ending with a WS row.**
Change to yarn C.
ROWS 33–34: **Rep rows 1 and 2 again, ending with a WS row.**
Change to yarn B.
ROW 35: **As row 1.**
Change to yarn A.
ROW 36: **As row 2.**
ROW 37: **As row 1.**
Change to yarn C.
ROW 38: **As row 2.**
ROW 39: **As row 1.**
ROW 40: **As row 2.**
Change to yarn B.
ROW 41: **As row 1.**
Change to yarn A.
ROW 42: **As row 2.**
ROWS 43–44: **Rep rows 1 and 2 once more.**
Change to yarn B.
ROW 45: **Knit.**
ROW 46: **Purl.**
These two rows form st st.
ROWS 47–60: **Rep last 2 rows seven more times, ending with a WS row.**

Change to yarn C.

ROW 61: **As row 45.**

ROW 62: **As row 46.**

Change to yarn B.

ROW 63: **As row 45.**

ROW 64: **As row 46.**

Change to yarn A.

ROW 65: **Knit.**

ROW 66: **Knit (this forms garter st ridge for turn over at top of bag).**

Change to yarn B.

ROWS 67–72: **Rep rows 45 and 46 three more times, ending with a WS row.**

Bind (cast) off.

Back

Using US 6 (4mm/no.8) needles and yarn A, cast on 50 sts.

ROW 1: **Knit.**

ROW 2: **K2, *p2, k2, rep from * to end.**

ROWS 3–24: **Rep rows 1 and 2 eleven more times, ending with a WS row.**

Change to yarn B.

ROWS 25–28: **Rep rows 1 and 2 twice more.**

Change to yarn A.

ROWS 29–30: **Rep rows 1 and 2, ending with a WS row.**

Change to yarn B.

ROWS 31–34: **Rep rows 1 and 2 twice more, ending with a WS row.**

ROW 35: **As row 1.**

Change to yarn A.

ROW 36: **As row 2.**

ROWS 37–44: **Rep rows 1 and 2 four more times, ending with a WS row.**

Change to yarn B.

ROW 45: **Knit.**

ROW 46: **Purl.**

These two rows form st st.

ROWS 47–60: **Rep last 2 rows seven more times, ending with a WS row.**

Change to yarn C.

ROW 61: **As row 45.**

ROW 62: **As row 46.**

Change to yarn B.

ROW 63: **As row 45.**

ROW 64: **As row 46.**

Change to yarn A.

ROW 65: **Knit.**

ROW 66: **Knit (this forms a garter st ridge for turn over at top of bag).**

Change to yarn B.

ROWS 67–72: **Rep rows 45 and 46 three more times, ending with a WS row.**

Bind (cast) off.

Handles (make 2)

Using US 6 (4mm/no.8) needles and yarn A, cast on 7 sts.

ROW 1: **Knit.**

ROW 2: **K1, p5, k1.**

Rep last 2 rows until handle measures 13¼in (34cm), ending with a WS row.

Bind (cast) off.

FINISHING

Sew in all the ends.

Using mattress stitch, join the Front and Back by working down one side, across the bottom and up the other side.

Fold down the turn at the top of the bag along the garter st ridge and using yarn A, slip stitch into place. Do this for both the Front and the Back.

Slip stitch handles securely in place approximately 1¼in (3cm) in from the side seams. Do this for the Front and Back.

Delight

This bag is full of life and offers a bit of everything—bobbles, stripes, beads, and even some sparkle. A balance is struck between the elaborate pattern on the front and the simple lines created with the use of stripes on the back.

SIZE

9in × 8¼in (23cm × 21cm), excluding handle

MATERIALS

1 pair US 6 (4mm/no.8) needles

Yarn

Rowan Handknit DK Cotton
1¾oz (50g) balls
    decadent (A)   2

Rowan 4-ply Soft
1¾oz (50g) balls
    buzz (B)   1
    (used double throughout)

Rowan Lurex Shimmer
1¾oz (50g) balls
    bedazzled (C)   1
    (used double throughout)

Beads

Jaeger
    mauve   approx. 120

GAUGE (TENSION)

20 sts and 28 rows to 4in (10cm) measured over pattern using US 6 (4mm/no.8) needles.

ABBREVIATIONS

beg	beginning
k	knit
mb	make bobble: using yarn B, (k1, p1) twice into next st, (turn, p4, turn, k4) twice, turn, p4, turn and sl2, k2tog, psso
p	purl
pb	place bead: yarn forward, slip bead to front of work, slip 1 st purlwise, take yarn to back of work. Bead will now be sitting in front of slipped stitch
rem	remaining
rep	repeat
RS	right side
st st	stockinette (stocking) stitch
sts	stitches
WS	wrong side

TECHNIQUES

Knitting with beads, see page 120
Sewing in ends, see page 118
Sewing up, see page 125

KNIT

Front

Using US 6 (4mm/no.8) needles and yarn A, cast on 50 sts.
ROW 1: Knit.
ROW 2–10: As row 1, ending with a WS row.
Change to yarn B.
ROW 11: As row 1.
ROW 12: Purl.
Change to yarn A.

ROWS 13–14: As rows 11 and 12, ending with a WS row.
Change to yarn C.
ROW 15: As row 1.
Change to yarn A.
ROW 16: As row 12.
ROW 17: K2, *mb, k2, rep from * to end.
ROW 18: As row 12.
Change to yarn C.
ROW 19: As row 1.
Change to yarn A.
ROW 20: As row 12.
ROW 21: K2, (pb, k1) to end.
ROW 22: As row 12.
Change to yarn B.
ROW 23: As row 1.

ROW 24: As row 12.
Change to yarn C.
ROW 25: As row 1.
Change to yarn A.
ROWS 26–28: As rows 20–22.
Change to yarn B.
ROWS 29–30: As rows 23–24.
Change to yarn C.
ROWS 31–32: As rows 23–24.
Change to yarn B.
ROWS 33–34: As rows 23–24.

Change to yarn A.

ROW 35–36: **As rows 23–24.**

ROW 37: **As row 21.**

ROW 38: **Purl.**

ROW 39: **As row 21.**

ROW 40: **Purl.**

Change to yarn C.

ROW 41: **Knit.**

Change to yarn B.

ROW 42: **Purl.**

ROW 43: **Knit.**

ROW 44: **Purl.**

ROWS 45–48: **Rep rows 43–44, ending with a WS row.**

Change to yarn A.

ROW 49: **Knit.**

ROW 50: **Purl.**

ROWS 51–52: **rep last 2 rows.**

ROW 53: **Knit.**

Change to yarn C.

ROW 54: **Purl.**

Change to yarn A.

ROW 55: **Knit.**

ROW 56: **Purl.**

ROW 57: **As row 21.**

ROW 58: **Purl.**

Change to yarn C.

ROW 59: **Knit.**

Change to yarn A.

ROW 60: **Purl.**

ROW 61: **Knit.**

ROWS 62–66: **Knit (row 66 creates a garter st ridge for turn over at top of bag).**

Change to yarn B.

ROW 67: **Knit.**

ROW 68: **Purl.**

ROWS 69–72: **Rep rows 67–68, ending with a WS row.**

Bind (cast) off.

Back

Using US 6 (4mm/no.8) needles and yarn A, cast on 50 sts.

ROW 1: **Knit.**

ROW 2–10: **As row 1, ending with a WS row.**

Change to yarn B.

ROW 11: **As row 1.**

ROW 12: **Purl.**

Change to yarn A.

ROWS 13–22: **As rows 11 and 12, ending with a WS row.**

Change to yarn B.

ROWS 23–24: **As rows 11 and 12.**

Change to yarn A.

ROWS 25–40: **As rows 11 and 12.**

Change to yarn B.

ROWS 41–48: **As rows 11 and 12.**

Change to yarn A.

ROWS 49–60: **As rows 11 and 12.**

ROW 61: **As row 11.**

ROWS 62–66: **Knit (row 66 creates garter st ridge for turn over at top of bag).**

Change to yarn B.

ROW 67: **Knit.**

ROW 68: **Purl.**

ROWS 69–72: **Rep rows 67–68, ending with a WS row.**

Bind (cast) off.

Front Handles (make 2)

Using US 6 (4mm/no.8) needles and yarn A, cast on 7 sts.

ROW 1: **Knit.**

ROW 2: **K1, p5, k1.**

Rep last 2 rows until handle measures 34cm/13½in, ending with a WS row.

Bind (cast) off.

FINISHING

Sew in all the ends.

Using mattress stitch, join the Front and Back by working down one side, across the bottom and up the other side.

Fold down the turn over at the top of the bag along the garter st ridge and, using yarn B, slip stitch into place. Do this for the Front and the Back.

Using yarn A, slip stitch handles securely in place approximately ¾in (2cm) in from the side seams. Do this for the Front and Back.

Helter–Skelter

In this design, lurex and tweed collide to create a very distinctive bag. The bold tucks provide a three-dimensional feel, which helps bring the bag to life. The shimmering lurex adjacent to the felted tweed is a dashing mix of textures that you will want to touch.

SIZE
8in x 8½in (20cm x 22cm), excluding handle

MATERIALS
1 pair US 7 (4.5mm/no.7) needles

Yarn
Rowan Felted Tweed
1¾oz (50g) balls
    watery (A)   2
    (used double throughout)

Rowan Lurex Shimmer
1oz (25g) balls
    minty (B)   1
    (used double throughout)

GAUGE (TENSION)
19 sts and 25 rows to 4in (10cm) measured over pattern using US 7 (4.5mm/no.7) needles.

ABBREVIATIONS
beg	beginning
cont	continue
k	knit
p	purl
rem	remaining
RS	right side
st st	stockinette (stocking) stitch
sts	stitches
WS	wrong side

TECHNIQUES
Sewing in ends, see page 118
Sewing up, see page 125

KNIT
Front
Using US 7 (4.5mm/no.7) needles and yarn A, cast on 39 sts.
ROW 1: **Knit.**
ROW 2: **(k3, p3) to last 3 sts, k3.**
ROWS 3–8: **Rep rows 1 and 2** three more times, ending with a WS row.
Change to yarn B.
ROW 9: **Knit.**
ROW 10: **Purl.**
ROWS 11–16: **Rep rows 9 and 10 three more times,** ending with a WS row.
ROW 17: **Still using yarn B, knit** the row of stitches on the left needle together with the 8th row below to create a tuck as follows: Insert needle through first st on left-hand needle and then through the first st on the 8th row below and knit together. Cont in this way until the whole of the current row has been knitted together with the 8th row below.
Change to yarn A.
ROW 12: **Purl.**
ROWS 13–20: **Rep rows 1 and 2** four more times, ending with a WS row.
ROWS 21–56: **Rep rows 9 to 20** three more times, ending with a WS row.

ROWS 57–59: **Rep rows 9 to 11 once more, ending with a RS row.**
ROW 60: **Still using yarn B, knit (this creates a garter st ridge for turn over at top of bag).**
Change to yarn A.
ROW 61: **Knit.**
ROW 62: **Purl.**
ROWS 63–66: **Rep last 2 rows twice more, ending with a WS row.**
Bind (cast) off.

Back
Using US 7 (4.5mm/no.7) needles and yarn A, cast on 39 sts.
ROW 1: **Knit.**
ROW 2: **(k3, p3) to last 3 sts, k3.**
ROWS 3–8: **Rep the last 2 rows three more times, ending with a WS row.**
Change to yarn B.
ROW 9: **Knit.**
ROW 10: **Purl.**
ROWS 11–50: **Rep rows 1 to 10 four more times, ending with a WS row.**
ROW 51: **Still using yarn B, knit.**
ROW 52: **Knit (this creates a garter st ridge for turn over at top of bag).**
Change to yarn A.
ROW 53: **Knit.**
ROW 54: **Purl.**
ROWS 55–58: **Rep last 2 rows twice more, ending with a WS row.**
Bind (cast) off.

Handles (make 2)
Using US 7 (4.5mm/no.7) needles and yarn A, cast on 7 sts.
ROW 1: **Knit.**
ROW 2: **K1, p5, k1,**
Rep last 2 rows until handle measures 11¾in (30cm), ending with a WS row.
Bind (cast) off.

FINISHING
Sew in all the ends.

Using mattress stitch, join the Front and Back by working down one side, across the bottom and up the other side.

Fold down the turn over at the top of the bag along the garter st ridge and, using yarn A, slip stitch into place. Do this for the Front and the Back.

Slip stitch handles securely in place approximately 1¼in (3cm) in from the side seams. Do this for the Front and Back.

Marina

Denim is used to full effect when the knit is as textured as possible to highlight the wonderful fading that occurs with washing. This bag uses all-over cables and seed (moss) stitch, which are enhanced with that first wash. This is a robust bag that will age gracefully.

SIZE
8¼in × 12in (21cm × 30cm)

MATERIALS
1 pair US 6 (4mm/no.8) needles

Yarn
Rowan Denim
1¾oz (50g) balls
    Nashville   3

GAUGE (TENSION)
Before washing
20 sts and 28 rows to 4in (10cm) measured over stockinette (stocking) stitch using US 6 (4mm/no.8) needles.
After washing
20 sts and 32 rows to 4in (10cm) measured over stockinette (stocking) stitch using US 6 (4mm/no.8) needles.

ABBREVIATIONS
beg	beginning
cont	continue
c6b	cable 6 back: slip next 3 sts onto a cable needle and hold at back of work, k3, then k3 from the cable needle
k	knit
p	purl
rem	remaining
rep	repeat
RS	right side
st st	stockinette (stocking) stitch
sts	stitches
WS	wrong side

TECHNIQUES
Sewing up, see page 125

KNIT
Front
Using US 6 (4mm/no.8) needles, cast on 54 sts.
ROW 1: (K1, p1) twice, k1, p2, k1, p1, *k6, p1, k1, p2, k1, p2, k1, p1 rep from * to last 15 sts, k6, p1, k1, p2, (k1, p1) twice, k1.

ROW 2: (K1, p1) four times, k1, *p6, (k1, p1) four times, k1, rep from * to last 15 sts, p6, k1, (p1, k1) to end.
ROWS 3–6: Rep last 2 rows, ending with a WS row.

TIP

When binding (casting) off and then casting on again on the next row to make the handle, it is like making a big buttonhole. To avoid the annoying loop that you can sometimes get in the corner of a buttonhole, on row 86, when you have to cast on 22 sts in between the 21st and the 22nd cast-on sts, bring the yarn to the front so it is trapped between the two.

ROW 7: (k1, p1) twice, k1, p2, k1, p1,
*c6b, p1, k1, p2, k1, p2, k1, p1, rep
from * to last 15 sts, c6b, p1, k1,
p2, (k1, p1) twice, k1.
ROWS 8–74: Rep rows 2–7 eleven
more times, then row 2 again,
ending with a WS row.
ROW 75: Knit.
ROW 76: Knit.
ROW 77: Knit.
ROW 78: Purl.
ROWS 79–84: Rep last 2 rows,
ending with a WS row.
ROW 85: K16, bind (cast) off center
22 sts, k to end.
ROW 86: P16, turn, cast on center
22 sts (see Tip), turn, p to end.
ROWS 87–94: As rows 77–78, ending
with a WS row.
Bind (cast) off.

Back
Using US 6 (4mm/no.8) needles,
cast on 54 sts.
ROW 1: (K1, p1) twice, k1, p2, k1, p1,
*k6, p1, k1, p2, k1, p2, k1, p1, rep
from * to last 15 sts, k6, p1, k1, p2,
(k1, p1) twice, k1.
ROW 2: (K1, p1) three times, k1, p1,
k1 *p6 (k1, p1) four times, k1 rep
from * to last 15 sts, p6, k1 (p1, k1)
to end.
ROWS 3–74: Rep last 2 rows, ending
with a WS row.
ROW 75: Knit.
ROW 76: Knit.
ROW 77: Knit.
ROW 78: Purl.
ROWS 79–84: Rep last 2 rows,
ending with a WS row.
ROW 85: K16, bind (cast) off center

22 sts, k to end.
ROW 86: p16, turn, cast on center
22 sts (see Tip), turn, p to end.
ROWS 87–94: as rows 77–78, ending
with a WS row.
Bind (cast) off.

FINISHING
Sew in all the ends.
    As Denim shrinks in length
when washed for the first time,
the Front, Back and enough yarn
to sew up with must all be
washed following the instructions
on the ball band before the bag is
sewn together.
    Using mattress stitch, join the
Front and Back by working down
one side, across the bottom and
up the other side.

Raspberry Milkshake

Texture is the key to the success of this bag. The first thing you will want to do is touch it! The contrast in texture is achieved not only through the use of bobbles against stockinette (stocking) stitch, but also through the use of a smooth yarn against the tweed.

SIZE
11½in × 11in (29cm × 28cm), excluding handle

MATERIALS
1 pair US 7 (4.5mm/no.7) needles

Yarn
Rowan Summer Tweed
1¾oz (50g) balls
    brilliant (A)   2

Rowan All Seasons Cotton
1¾oz (50g) balls
    giddy (B)   2

GAUGE (TENSION)
18 sts and 25 rows to 4in (10cm) measured over pattern using US 7 (4.5mm/no.7) needles.

ABBREVIATIONS
beg	beginning
k	knit
mb	make bobble: using yarn B, (k1, p1) twice into next st, (turn, p4, turn, k4) twice, turn, p4, turn and sl2, k2tog, psso
p	purl
rem	remaining
rep	repeat
RS	right side
st st	stockinette (stocking) stitch
sts	stitches
Ws	wrong side

TECHNIQUES
Sewing in ends, see page 118
Sewing up, see page 125

KNIT
Front
Using US 7 (4.5mm/no.7) needles and yarn A, cast on 55 sts.
ROW 1: **Knit.**
ROW 2: **Purl.**
These two rows form st st.
ROWS 3–42: **Work from chart in st st, beg with a knit (RS) row and as follows: work rows 3–22, then rep rows 7–22, and then rows 7–10, ending with a WS row.**
Change to yarn B.
ROW 43: **Knit.**
ROW 44: **Purl.**
ROWS 45–46: **Rep last 2 rows.**
Change to yarn A.
ROWS 47–74: **Work from chart in st st, beg with a knit (RS) row and ending with a purl (WS) row as follows: work rows 9–22, then rep rows 7–20, ending with a WS row.**
Change to yarn B.
ROWS 75–76: **As rows 43 and 44.**
ROW 77: **As row 43**
ROW 78: **Knit (this creates garter st ridge for turn over at top of bag).**
Change to yarn A.
ROWS 79–82: **As rows 43 and 44, ending with a WS row.**
Bind (cast) off.

Back
Using US 7 (4.5mm/no.7) needles and yarn A, cast on 55 sts.

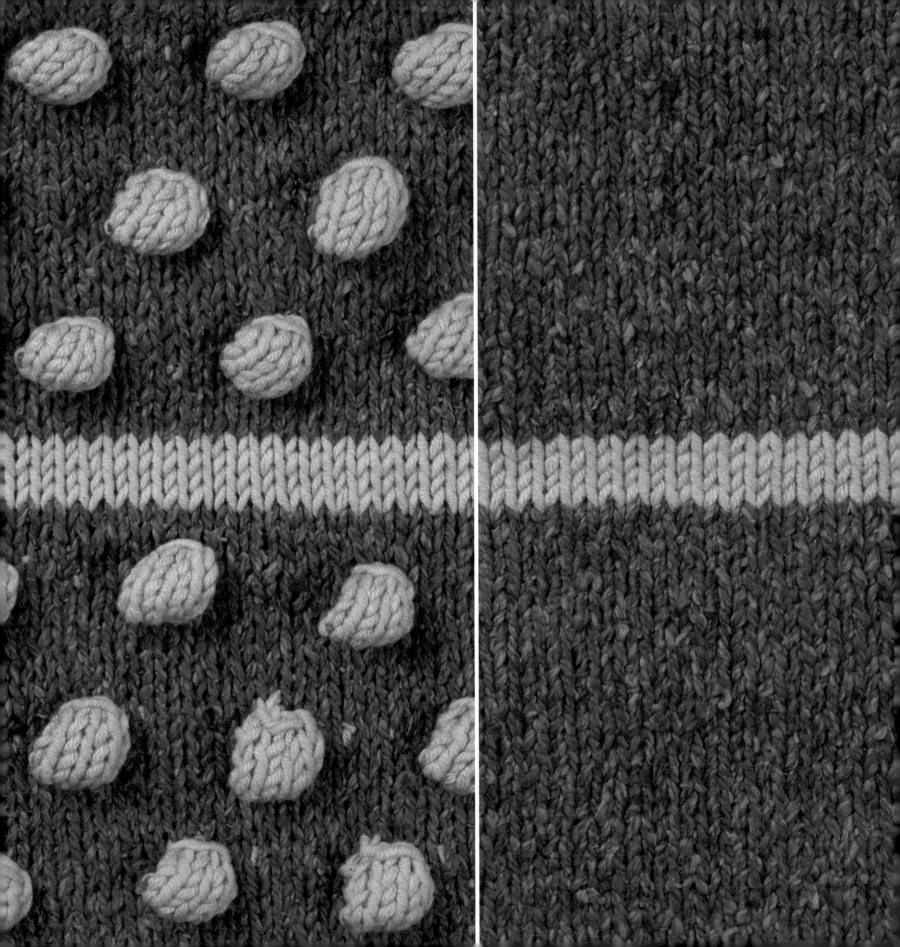

CHART

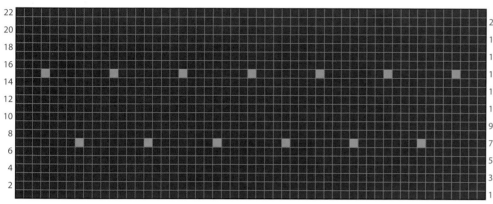

Key

■ brilliant (A)

■ mb

ROW 1: **Knit.**
ROW 2: **Purl.**
ROWS 3–42: **As rows 1 and 2, ending with a WS row.**
Change to yarn B.
ROW 43–46: **As rows 1 and 2.**
Change to yarn A.
ROWS 47–74: **As rows 1 and 2.**
Change to yarn B.
ROWS 75–76: **As rows 1 and 2.**
ROW 77: **As row 1.**
ROW 78: **Knit (this creates garter st ridge for turn over at top of bag).**
Change to yarn A.
ROWS 79–82: **As rows 1 and 2, ending with a WS row.**
Bind (cast) off.

Handles (make 2)

Using US 7 (4.5mm/no.7) needles and yarn A, cast on 7 sts.
ROW 1: **Knit.**
ROW 2: **K1, p5, k1.**
Rep last 2 rows until handle measures 18¼in (46cm).

FINISHING

Sew in all the ends.

Using mattress stitch, join the Front and Back by working down one side, across the bottom and up the other side.

Fold down the turn at the top of the bag along the garter st ridge and, using yarn A, slip stitch into place. Do this for both the Front and the Back.

Slip stitch handles securely in place approximately 1in (2.5cm) in from the side seams. Do this for the Front and Back.

Bon-Bon

Here is a simple, textured knit with seed (moss) stitch detail around the top. The contrasting handles sewn to each side of the bag make a lively addition to the garter stitch body. Not many of my bags have the same front and back—this one does, rendering it super-speedy to knit.

SIZE
11in × 6¼in (28cm × 16cm), excluding handle

MATERIALS
1 pair US 9 (5.5mm/no.5) needles

Yarn
Rowan Handknit DK Cotton
1¾oz (50g) balls
  gooseberry (A) 2
  (used double throughout)
  zing (B) 1
  (used double throughout)

Rowan Kid Silk Haze
1oz (25g) balls
  jelly (C) 1
  (used quadruple throughout)

GAUGE (TENSION)
15½ sts and 21 rows to 4in (10cm) measured over garter stitch using US 9 (5.5mm/no.5) needles.

ABBREVIATIONS
beg   beginning
k   knit
p   purl
rem   remaining
rep   repeat
RS   right side
st st stockinette (stocking) stitch
sts   stitches
WS   wrong side

TECHNIQUES
Sewing up, see page 125

KNIT
Front and Back alike
Using US 9 (5.5mm/no.5) needles and yarn A, cast on 41 sts.
ROW 1: **Knit.**
This row forms garter st.
ROWS 2–32: **As row 1,** ending with a WS row.
Change to yarn C.
ROW 33: **K1, *p1, k1, rep from * to end.**
This row forms seed (moss) st.
ROW 34: **As row 33.**
Change to yarn B.
ROW 35: **As row 33.**
Change to yarn A.
ROW 36: **As row 33.**
Change to yarn B.

ROWS 37–38: **As row 33.**
Change to yarn A.
ROWS 39–40: **Knit (row 40 creates a
garter st ridge for turn over at top
of bag).**
ROW 41: **Knit.**
ROW 42: **Purl.**
ROWS 43–48: **As rows 41–42, ending
with a WS row.
Bind (cast) off.**

Handles (make 2)
Using US 9 (5.5mm/no.5) needles
and yarn B, cast on 5 sts.
ROW 1: **Knit.**
ROW 2: **K1, p3, k1.**
Rep last 2 rows until handle
measures 11¾in (30cm), ending
with a WS row.
Bind (cast) off.

FINISHING
Sew in all the ends.
　　Using mattress stitch, join the
Front and Back by working down
one side, across the bottom and
up the other side.
　　Fold down the turn over at the
top of the bag along the garter st
ridge and, using yarn A, slip stitch
into place. Do this for the Front
and the Back.
　　Slip stitch handles securely in
place on the outside of bag 2½in
(6cm) from side seams.

Bubbles

Shades of blue and turquoise combine with bobbles to give a distinctly watery feel to this little number. The bead detail at the top of the bag reflects that of the bobbles underneath, a witty combination that simultaneously adds just a hint of sparkle.

SIZE

6¼in x 8¾in (16cm x 22cm), excluding handle

MATERIALS

1 pair US 6 (4mm/no.8) needles

Yarn

Rowan Handknit DK Cotton
1¾oz (50g) balls
    diana (A)   2

Rowan Wool Cotton
1¾oz (50g) balls
    aqua (B)   1

Beads

    turquoise   approx. 17

GAUGE (TENSION)

21 sts and 27 rows to 4in (10cm) measured over stockinette (stocking) stitch using US 6 (4mm/no.8) needles.

ABBREVIATIONS

beg	beginning
k	knit
mb	make bobble as follows: using yarn B knit and purl into next st (2sts), turn, purl 2, turn, sl1, k1, psso
p	purl
pb	place bead: yarn forward, slip bead to front of work, slip 1 st purlwise, take yarn to back of work. Bead will now be sitting in front of the slipped stitch
rem	remaining
RS	right side
st st	stockinette (stocking) stitch
sts	stitches
WS	wrong side

TECHNIQUES

Knitting with beads, see page 120
Sewing in ends, see page 118
Sewing up, see page 125

KNIT

Front

Using US 6 (4mm/no.8) needles and yarn A, cast on 37 sts.
ROW 1 (RS): Knit.
ROW 2 (WS): Purl.
These last 2 rows form st st.
ROWS 3–52: Work from chart 1 (see page 61) in st st, beg with a RS row as follows:
Work rows 3–18, then rep rows 7–18 twice and then rows 7–16, ending with a WS row.

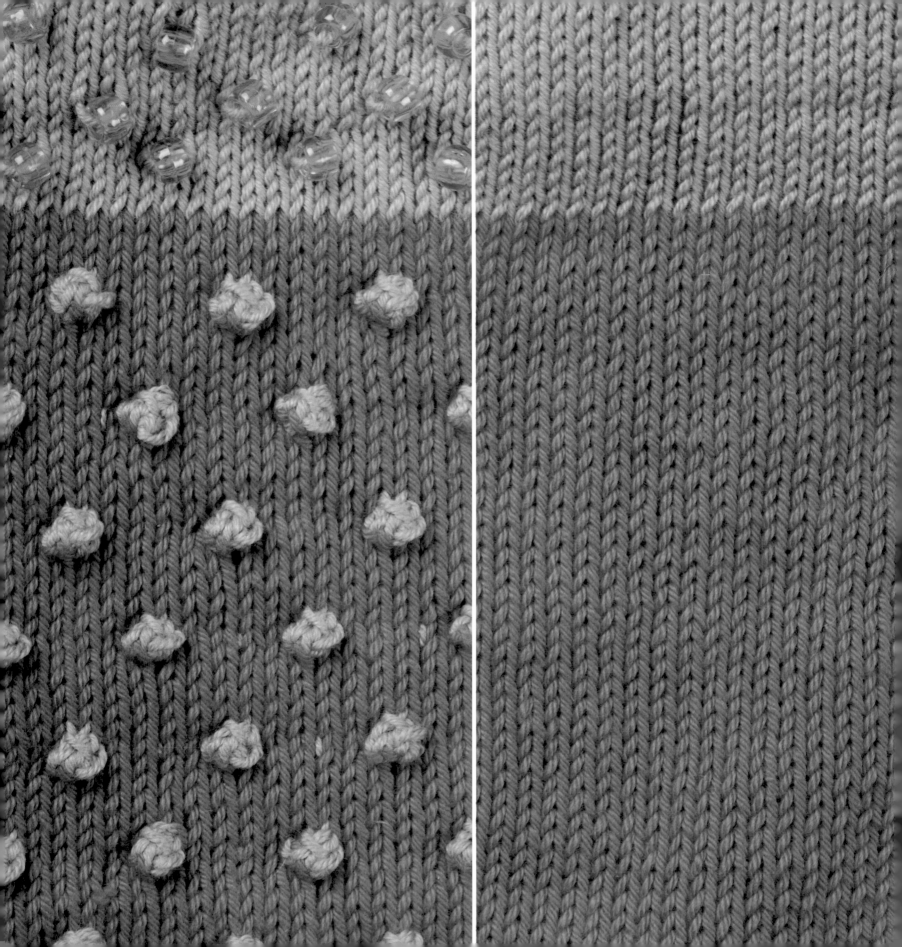

Change to yarn B.

ROWS 53–66: **Work from chart 2 in st st, beg with a RS row as follows:**

Work rows 1–12, then rep rows 5–6, ending with a WS row.

Change to yarn A.

ROW 67: **Knit.**

ROW 68: **Knit (this creates a garter st ridge for turn over at top of bag).**

Change to yarn B.

ROW 69: **Knit.**

ROW 70: **Purl.**

ROWS 71–76: **Rep last 2 rows, ending with a WS row.**

Bind (cast) off.

Back

Using US 6 (4mm/no.8) needles and yarn A, cast on 37 sts.

ROW 1: **Knit.**

ROW 2: **Purl.**

ROWS 3–52: **Rep last 2 rows, ending with a WS row.**

Change to yarn B.

ROWS 53–66: **Rep rows 1 and 2, ending with a WS row.**

Change to yarn A.

ROW 67: **Knit.**

ROW 68: **Knit (this creates a garter st ridge for turn over at top of bag).**

Change to yarn B.

ROW 69: **Knit.**

ROW 70: **Purl.**

ROWS 71–76: **Rep last 2 rows, ending with a WS row.**

Bind (cast) off.

Handles (make 2)

Using US 6 (4mm/no.8) needles and yarn A, cast on 7 sts.

ROW 1: **Knit.**

ROW 2: **K1, p5, k1.**

Rep last 2 rows until handle measures 9½in (24cm), ending with a WS row.

Bind (cast) off.

FINISHING

Sew in all the ends.

Using mattress stitch, join the Front and Back by working down one side, across the bottom and up the other side.

Fold down the turn over at the top of the bag along the garter st ridge and, using yarn A, slip stitch into place. Do this for the front and the back.

Slip stitch handles securely in place approximately 1in (2.5cm) in from the side seams. Do this for the front and back.

CHART 1

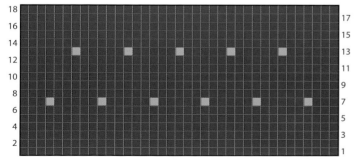

Key

■ diana (A)

□ mb

CHART 2

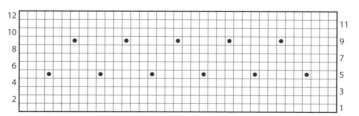

Key

□ aqua (B)

☉ pb

Ocean

I live by the sea, which provided the inspiration for this bag. A range of blues crash and collide together to create an elegant bag with a bit of shimmer, thanks to the lurex. The bag uses tweeds, which feature a medley of colors conjured up by a summer's day at the beach.

SIZE
10in x 9¾in (25cm x 24cm), excluding handle

MATERIALS
1 pair US 8 (5mm/no.6) needles
1 pair US 7 (4.5mm/no.7) needles

Yarn
Rowan Summer Tweed
1¾oz (50g) balls
   exotic (A)   1

Rowan Cotton Glacé
1¾oz (50g) balls
   pier (B)   1
   (used double throughout)

Rowan Lurex Shimmer
1oz (25g) balls
   minty (C)   1
   (used double throughout)

GAUGE (TENSION)
18 sts and 23 rows to 4in (10cm) measured over pattern using US 7 (4.5mm/no.7) needles.

ABBREVIATIONS
beg	beginning
k	knit
p	purl
rem	remaining
rep	repeat
RS	right side
st st	stockinette (stocking) st
sts	stitches
WS	wrong side

TECHNIQUES
Fair Isle, see page 119
Sewing in ends, see page 118
Sewing up, see page 125

KNIT
Front
Using US 7 (4.5mm/no.7) needles and yarn A, cast on 49 sts.
ROW 1: Knit.
ROW 2: Purl.
These 2 rows form st st.
ROWS 3–6: Rep rows 1 and 2 twice more, ending with a WS row.
Change to yarn B.
ROW 7–8: Rep rows 1 and 2.
Change to yarn A.
ROW 9: As row 1.
Change to yarn C.
ROW 10: As row 2.
Change to yarn B.
ROW 11: As row 1.
Change to yarn A.
ROW 12: As row 2.
ROWS 13–16: Rep rows 1 and 2 twice more, ending with a WS row.
Change to yarn C.
ROW 17: As row 1.
Change to yarn A.
ROW 18: As row 2.
ROWS 19–22: Rep rows 1 and 2 twice more, ending with a WS row.
Change to yarn B.
ROW 23–24: Rep row 1 and 2, ending with a WS row.
Change to yarn A.
ROW 25: As row 1.
Change to yarn C.
ROW 26: As row 2.
Change to yarn B.

ROW 27: As row 1.
Change to yarn A.
ROW 28: As row 2.
ROWS 29–32: Rep rows 1 and 2 twice more, ending with a WS row.
ROWS 33–43: Work 11 rows from chart in st st and using the Fair Isle technique described on page 119, beg with a RS row and ending with a RS row.
Change to yarn A.
ROW 44: (WS) As row 2.

ROWS 45–46: Rep rows 1 and 2 once more, ending with a WS row.
ROW 47 (RS) (CREATES HANDLE): k13, bind (cast) off center 23 sts, k to end.
ROW 48 (WS): P13, turn, cast on center 23 sts, turn, p to end.
ROWS 49–54: Rep rows 1 and 2 three times, ending with a WS row.
Bind (cast) off.

CHART

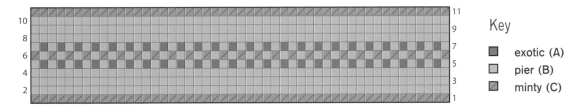

Key

■ exotic (A)
■ pier (B)
▨ minty (C)

Back

Using US 7 (4.5mm/no.7) needles and yarn A, cast on 49 sts.

ROW 1: **Knit.**

ROW 2: **Purl.**

These 2 rows form st st.

ROWS 3–6: **Rep rows 1 and 2 twice more, ending with a WS row.**

Change to yarn B.

ROWS 7–10: **Rep rows 1 and 2 twice more.**

ROW 11: **As row 1.**

Change to yarn A.

ROW 12: **As row 2.**

ROWS 13–22: **Rep rows 1 and 2 five times, ending with a WS row.**

Change to yarn B.

ROWS 23–26: **Rep rows 1 and 2 twice more.**

ROW 27: **As row 1.**

Change to yarn A.

ROW 28: **As row 2.**

ROWS 29–32: **Rep rows 1 and 2 twice more, ending with a WS row.**

Change to yarn C.

ROW 33: **As row 1.**

Change to yarn B.

ROW 34: **As row 2.**

ROWS 35–42: **Rep rows 1 and 2 four times, ending with a WS row.**

Change to yarn C.

ROW 43: **As row 1.**

Change to yarn A.

ROW 44 (WS): **As row 2.**

ROWS 45–46: **Rep rows 1 and 2 once more, ending with a WS row.**

ROW 47 (RS) (CREATES HANDLE): **K13, bind (cast) off center 23 sts, k to end.**

ROW 48 (WS): **P13, turn, cast on center 23 sts, turn, p to end.**

ROWS 49–54: **Rep rows 1 and 2 three times, ending with a WS row.**

Bind (cast) off.

FINISHING

Sew in all the ends.

Using mattress stitch, join the Front and Back by working down one side, across the bottom and up the other side.

Children's bags

Camouflage

Here is a practical drawstring rucksack designed to accompany any inquisitive youngster off on an adventure. There is plenty of room to store the treasures collected along the way! The intarsia is a patch pocket and the drawstrings make it very easy to carry around.

SIZE
9¾in x 11in (24cm x 28cm)

MATERIALS
1 pair US 7 (4.5mm/no.7) needles

Yarn
Rowan All Seasons Cotton
1¾oz (50g) balls

military (A)	2
fern (B)	1
limedrop (C)	1

GAUGE (TENSION)
18 sts and 25 rows to 4in (10cm) measured over pattern using US 7 (4.5mm/no.7) needles.

ABBREVIATIONS
beg	beginning
k	knit
p	purl
rem	remaining
rep	repeat
RS	right side
st st	stockinette (stocking) stitch
sts	stitches
WS	wrong side

TECHNIQUES
Intarsia, see page 118
Sewing in ends, see page 118
Sewing up, see page 125

KNIT
Front
Using US 7 (4.5mm/no.7) needles and yarn B, cast on 45 sts.
Change to yarn C.
ROW 1: Knit.
Change to yarn A.
ROWS 2–8: As row 1, ending with a WS row.
ROW 9 (EYELET ROW): K4, yf, k2tog, *k3, yf, k2tog, rep from * to last 4 sts, k4.
ROW 10: As row 1.
Change to yarn B.
ROWS 11–14: As row 1, ending with a WS row.
Change to yarn C.
ROW 15: Knit.
ROW 16: Purl.
These 2 rows form st st.
ROWS 17–18: Rep rows 15–16 once more, ending with a WS row.
Change to yarn B.
ROW 19: Knit.
Change to yarn A.
ROWS 20–34: Beg with a WS row, work 14 rows st st as set by rows 15 and 16, ending with a WS row. For rows 35–56 use the intarsia method as described on page 118.
ROW 35: K15 using yarn A, k15 using yarn C, knit to end using yarn A.
ROW 36: P15 using yarn A, p15 using yarn C, purl to end using yarn A.
ROWS 37–56: Rep rows 35–36 nine more times ending with a WS row.

Using only yarn A:
ROWS 57–76: Beg with a RS row, work twenty rows st st as set by rows 15 and 16, ending with a WS row.
Bind (cast) off.

CHART

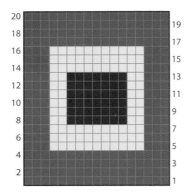

Key

- ■ military (A)
- ■ fern (B)
- □ limedrop (C)

Back

Using US 7 (4.5mm/no.7) needles and yarn B, cast on 45 sts.
Change to yarn C.

ROW 1: Knit.

Change to yarn A.

ROWS 2–8: As row 1, ending with a WS row.

ROW 9 (EYELET ROW): K4, yf, k2tog, *k3, yf, k2tog, rep from * to last 4 sts, k4.

ROW 10: Knit.

Change to yarn B.

ROWS 11–14: Knit, ending with a WS row.

Change to yarn C.

ROW 15: Knit.

ROW 16: Purl.

These 2 rows form st st.

ROWS 17–18: Rep rows 15–16.

Change to yarn B.

ROW 19: Knit.

ROWS 20–46: Beg with a WS row, work 27 rows st st as set by rows 15 and 16, ending with a WS row.

Change to yarn B.

ROWS 47–76: Beg with a RS row, work 29 rows st st as set by rows 15 and 16, ending with a WS row.

Bind (cast) off.

Pocket

Using US 7 (4.5mm/no.7) needles and yarn B, cast on 17 sts.
Using the intarsia method described on page 118, work 20 rows from chart in st st as set by rows 15–16 of Front, beg with a RS row and ending with WS row.

Still using yarn B:

ROW 21: Purl (this creates a garter st ridge for fold over at top of pocket).

Change to yarn C.

ROWS 22: Knit.

ROW 23: Purl.

Rep rows 22–23 four more times, ending with a WS row.

Bind (cast) off.

Twisted cord (make 2)

Cut two lengths of yarn B and two lengths of yarn C each approximately 10ft 3in (310cm) long. Take the four lengths of yarn and secure at each end with knots. Ask some one to help you and give them one end of the yarn while you hold the other. With the yarn

outstretched, each end needs to be twisted in opposite directions until it shows signs of twisting back on itself. Bring the two ends of the cord together and hold tightly, allowing the two halves to twist together. Smooth out any bumps by running your fingers up and down the cord. You will now have a twisted cord approximately 4ft 1in (124cm) long.

FINISHING

Sew in all the ends.

Fold down the turn over at the top of the pocket along the garter st ridge and, using yarn C, slip stitch into place. Slip st pocket into place on front of bag as shown in the photograph.

Using mattress stitch, join the Front and Back by working down one side, across the bottom and up the other side.

Thread the first twisted cord through the eyelets on the front of the bag and the second twisted cord through the eyelets on the back of the bag. Tie the two cords on the left-hand side together, trim the ends and then sew to the bottom left-hand corner of the bag neatly and securely. Tie the two cords on the right-hand side together and work as for left.

Loveheart

A pretty drawstring rucksack with plenty of room for all of the keepsakes a child collects. A cute pocket on the front uses simple intarsia to create the heart motif. The twisted cords are a fun feature and use different colors for a stripey finish.

SIZE
9in × 7½in (23cm × 19cm), excluding handle

MATERIALS
1 pair US 7 (4.5mm/no.7) needles

Yarn
Rowan All Seasons Cotton
1¾oz (50g) balls
giddy (A)   2

Rowan Cotton Glacé
1¾oz (50g) balls
  bubbles (B)   1
  (used double throughout)

Rowan Lurex Shimmer
1oz (25g) balls
  gleam (C)   1
  (used double throughout)

GAUGE (TENSION)
18 sts and 25 rows to 4in (10cm) measured over pattern using US 7 (4.5mm/no.7) needles.

ABBREVIATIONS
beg   beginning
k   knit
p   purl
rem   remaining
rep   repeat
RS   right side
st st   stockinette (stocking) stitch
sts   stitches
WS   wrong side

TECHNIQUES
Intarsia, see page 118
Sewing in ends, see page 118
Sewing up, see page 125

KNIT
Front
Using US 7 (4.5mm/no.7) needles and yarn C, cast on 45 sts.
Change to yarn B.
ROW 1: Knit.
Change to yarn A.
ROWS 2–8: As row 1, ending with a WS row.
ROW 9 (EYELET ROW): K4, yf, k2tog, *k3, yf, k2tog, rep from * to last 4 sts, k4.
ROW 10: As row 1.
Change to yarn B.
ROWS 11–14: As row 1, ending with a WS row.
Change to yarn C.
ROW 15: Knit.
ROW 16: Purl.
These 2 rows form st st.
ROWS 17–18: Rep last 2 rows once more, ending with a WS row.
Change to yarn A.
ROWS 19–34: Beg with a RS row, work 16 rows st st as set by rows 15 and 16, ending with a WS row. For rows 35–56 use the intarsia method as described on page 118.
ROW 35: K15 using yarn A, k15 using yarn B, knit to end using yarn A.
ROW 36: P15 using yarn A, p15 using yarn B, purl to end using yarn A.
ROWS 37–56: Rep last 2 rows ten more times, ending with a WS row. Using only yarn A.
ROWS 57–76: Beg with a RS row, work 20 rows st st as set by rows 15 and 16, ending with a WS row. Bind (cast) off.

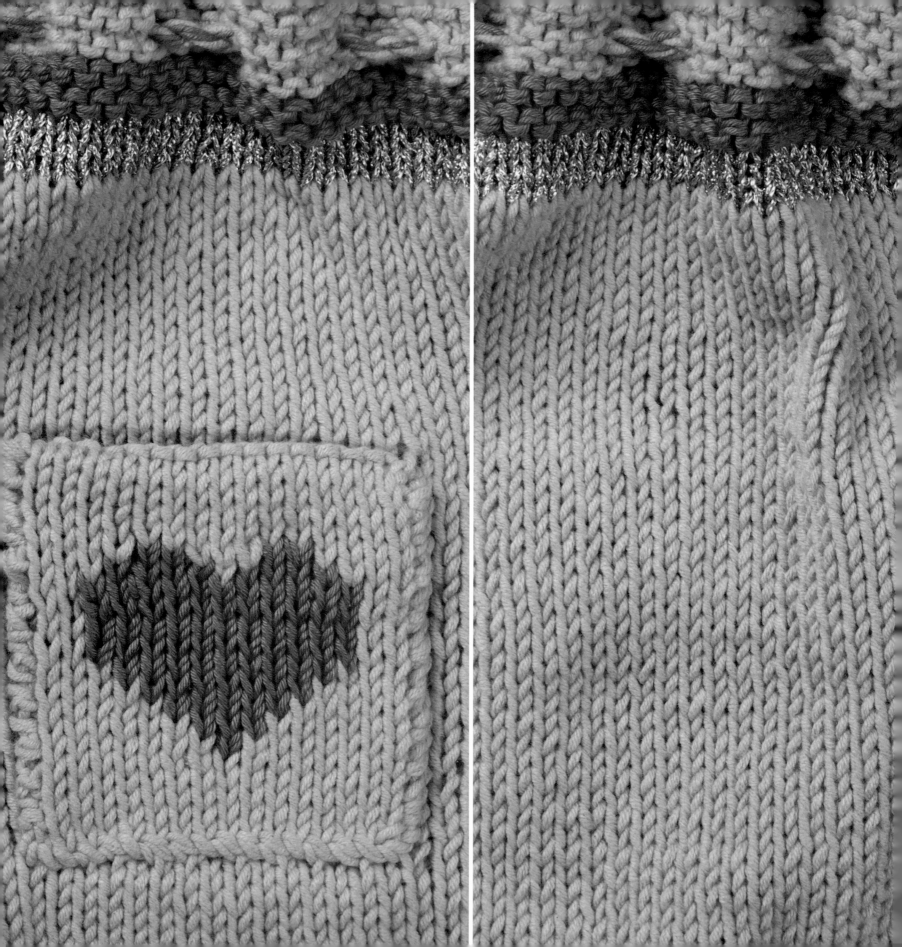

CHART

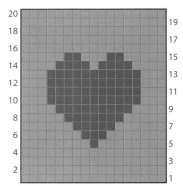

20
18
16
14
12
10
8
6
4
2

19
17
15
13
11
9
7
5
3
1

Key

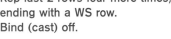
□ giddy (A)
■ bubbles (B)

Back

Using US 7 (4.5mm/no.7) needles and yarn C, cast on 45 sts.
Change to yarn B.
ROW 1: Knit.
Change to yarn A.
ROWS 2–8: As row 1, ending with a WS row.
ROW 9 (EYELET ROW): K4, yf, k2tog, *k3, yf, k2tog, rep from * to last 4 sts, k4.
ROW 10: As row 1.
Change to yarn B.
ROWS 11–14: As row 1, ending with a WS row.
Change to yarn C.
ROW 15: Knit.
ROW 16: Purl.
These 2 rows form st st.
ROWS 17–18: Rep last 2 rows once more, ending with a WS row.
ROWS 19–76: Beg with a RS row, work 58 rows st st as set by rows 15 and 16, ending with a WS row.
Bind (cast) off.

Pocket

Using US 7 (4.5mm/no.7) needles and yarn A, cast on 17 sts.
Using the intarsia method described on page 118, work 20 rows from chart in st st as set by rows 15–16 of Front, beg with a RS row and ending with WS row.
Still using yarn A:
ROW 21: Purl (this creates a garter st ridge for fold over at top of pocket).
Change to yarn B.
ROWS 22: Knit.
ROW 23: Purl.

Rep last 2 rows four more times, ending with a WS row.
Bind (cast) off.

Twisted cord (make 2)

Cut two lengths of yarn A and two lengths of yarn B, each approximately 10ft 3in (310cm) long. Take the four lengths of yarn and secure at each end with knots. Ask some one to help you and give them one end of the yarn while you hold the other. With the yarn outstretched, each end needs to be twisted in opposite directions until it shows signs of twisting back on itself. Bring the two ends of the cord together and hold tightly, allowing the two halves to twist together. Smooth out any bumps by running your fingers up and down the cord. You will now have a twisted cord approximately 4ft 1in (124cm) long.

FINISHING

Sew in all the ends.

Fold down the turn over at the top of the pocket along the garter st ridge and, using yarn B, slip stitch into place. Slip st pocket into place on Front of bag, as shown in the photograph.

Using mattress stitch, join the Front and Back by working down one side, across the bottom and up the other side.

Thread the first twisted cord through the eyelets on the front of the bag and the second twisted cord through the eyelets on the back of the bag. Tie the two cords on the left-hand side together, trim the ends and then sew to the bottom left-hand corner of the bag neatly and securely.

Tie together the two cords on the right-hand side and work as for the left.

Evening bags

Plum

Vertical and horizontal stripes are the main features of this bag while the shades of purple are lifted by accents of shiny lurex. A delicate twisted cord attached to the top of the bag for the handle provides a relief against the boldness of the knit itself.

SIZE
7¾in x 8in (19cm x 20cm), excluding handle

MATERIALS
1 pair US 9 (5.5mm/no.5) needles

Yarn
Rowan Cotton Glacé
1¾oz (50g) balls
    hyacinth (A)   2
    (used triple throughout)

Rowan Handknit DK Cotton
1¾oz (50g) balls
    lupin (B)   1
    (used double throughout)

Rowan Lurex Shimmer
1¾oz (50g) balls
    bedazzled (C)   1
    (used triple throughout)

Rowan Kid Classic
1¾oz (50g) balls
    royal (D)   1
    (used double throughout)

GAUGE (TENSION)
15½ sts and 21 rows to 4in (10cm) measured over stockinette (stocking) stitch using US 9 (5.5mm/no.5) needles.

ABBREVIATIONS
beg   beginning
k   knit
p   purl
sts   stitches
WS   wrong side

TECHNIQUES
Fair Isle, see page 119
Sewing in ends, see page 118
Sewing up, see page 125

KNIT
Front
Using US 9 (5.5mm/no.5) needles and yarn D, cast on 33 sts.
ROW 1: Knit.
ROW 2: Purl.
ROWS 3–4: As rows 1 and 2.
ROW 5: Knit.
Change to yarn C.
ROW 6: Purl.
Change to row B.
ROWS 7–10: As rows 1 and 2.
ROW 11: Knit.
Change to yarn A.
ROW 12: Purl.
ROW 13: Knit.

Change to yarn C.
ROW 14: Purl.
Change to yarn D.
ROWS 15–18: As rows 1 and 2.
ROW 19: Knit.
Change to yarn C.
ROW 20: Purl.
Change to yarn B.
ROWS 21–24: As rows 1 and 2.
ROW 25: Knit.
Change to yarn A.

ROW 26: Purl.
ROW 27: Knit.
Change to yarn B.
ROW 28: Purl.
Change to yarn C.
ROW 29: Knit.
Change to yarn D.
ROW 30: Purl.
ROW 31: Knit.
Change to yarn B.
ROWS 32–34: To be worked from

CHART

Key

■ lupin (B)

■ bedazzled (C)

---

chart using Fair Isle technique as described on page 119, ending with a WS row.

Change to yarn A.

ROW 35: Knit.

Change to yarn B.

ROWS 36–38: To be worked from chart using Fair Isle technique as described on page 119, ending with a WS row.

Change to yarn A.

ROWS 39–42: As rows 1 and 2.

ROW 43: Knit.

ROW 44: Knit (this creates garter st ridge for turn over at top of bag).

ROWS 45–48: As rows 1 and 2 , ending with a WS row.

Bind (cast) off.

Back

Using US 9 (5.5mm/no.5) needles cast on 11 sts using yarn D, 11 sts using yarn B and 11 sts using yarn A (33 sts).

Using intarsia method as described on page 118 continue as follows:

ROW 1: Knit.

ROW 2: Purl.

ROWS 3–32: As rows 1 and 2, ending with a WS row.

Break off yarns.

Change to yarn C.

ROW 33: Knit.

Change to yarn D.

ROW 34: Purl.

ROW 35: Knit.

ROWS 36–38: To be worked from chart, ending with a WS row.

Change to yarn A.

ROWS 39–42: As rows 1 and 2.

ROW 43: Knit.

ROW 44: Knit (this creates garter st ridge for turn over at top of bag).

ROWS 45–48: As rows 1 and 2, ending with a WS row.

Bind (cast) off.

Twisted cord

Cut three lengths of yarns A, B, C and D, each approximately 30in (75cm) long. Take the four lengths of yarn and secure at each end with knots. Ask some one to help you and give them one end of the yarn while you hold the other. With the yarn outstretched, each end needs to be twisted in opposite directions until it shows signs of twisting back on itself. Bring the two ends of the cord together and hold tightly, allowing the two halves to twist together. Smooth out any bumps by running your fingers up and down the cord. You will now have a twisted cord approximately 12in (30cm) long.

FINISHING

Sew in all the ends.

Using mattress stitch, join the Front and Back by working down one side, across the bottom and up the other side.

Fold down the turn over at the top of the bag along the garter st ridge and, using yarn A, slip stitch into place.

Sew handle neatly and securely to inside of side seams at top of bag.

Twilight

This dainty drawstring purse gleams and twinkles as it catches the light. The lurex yarn used for the base reflects the sequin detail at the top. For something a little brighter, choose different colored lurex or sequins. Any bright shade combines well with navy.

SIZE
6¼in x 8in (16cm x 20cm)

MATERIALS
1 pair US 3 (3.25mm/no.10) needles

Yarn
Rowan 4-ply Soft
1¾oz (50g) balls
    marine (A)   1

Rowan Lurex Shimmer
1oz (25g) balls
    midnight (B)   2

Sequins
    navy   approx. 45

GAUGE (TENSION)
29 sts and 41 rows to 4in (10cm) measured over stockinette (stocking) stitch US 3 (3.25mm/no.10) needles.

ABBREVIATIONS
beg	beginning
k	knit
k2tog	knit 2 stitches together
p	purl
rem	remaining
RS	right side
st st	stockinette (stocking) stitch
sts	stitches
Ws	wrong side
yf	yarn forward

TECHNIQUES
Knitting with sequins, see page 122
Sewing in ends, see page 118
Sewing up, see page 125

KNIT
Front
Using US 3 (3.25mm/no.10) needles and yarn B, cast on 49 sts.
Change to yarn A.
ROW 1: K1, *p1, k1, rep from * to end.
This row forms seed (moss) stitch.
ROWS 2–6: Rep row 1, ending with a WS row.
ROW 7: K3, *yf, k2tog, K4, rep from * to last 4 sts, yf, k2tog, k2.
ROW 8: Purl.
Change to yarn B.
ROW 9: Knit.
Change to yarn A.
ROWS 10–24: Work 15 rows from chart (overleaf) in st st to place sequins, beg with a purl (WS) row and ending with knit (RS) row.

Change to yarn B.
ROW 25: Knit.
ROW 26: Purl.
ROWS 27–82: As rows 25–26, ending with a WS row.
Bind (cast) off.

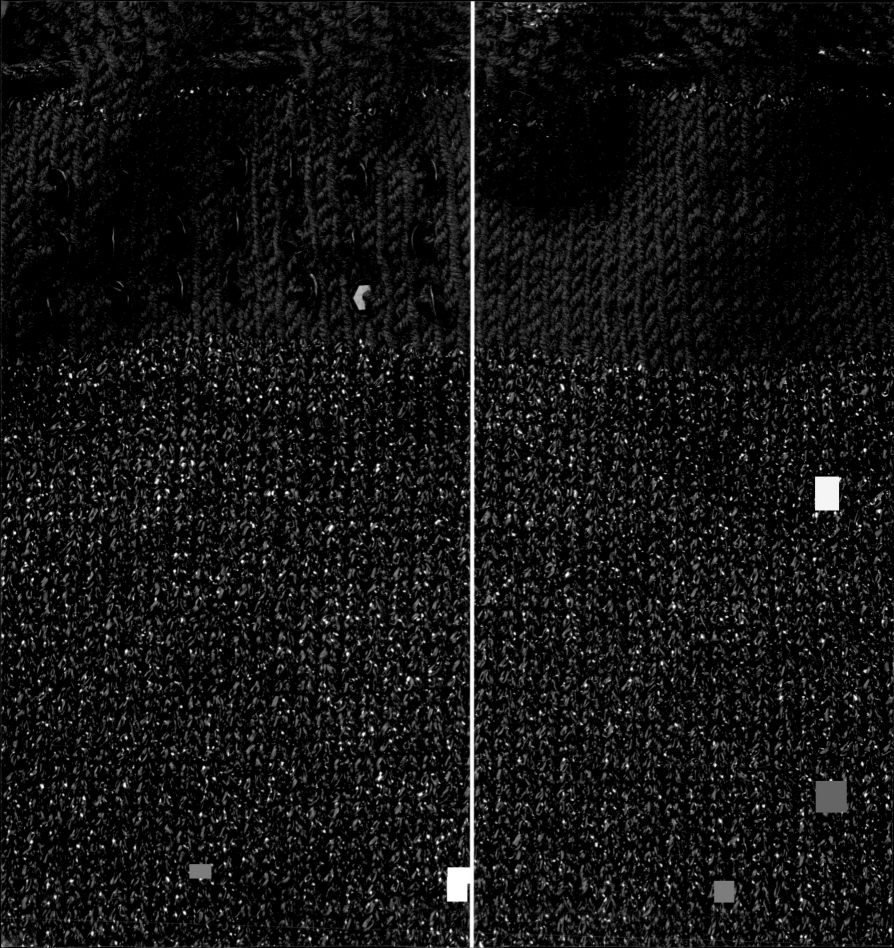

Back

Using US 3 (3.25mm/no.10) needles and yarn B, cast on 49 sts.
Change to yarn A.
ROWS 1–9: Work as for Front.
Change to yarn A.
ROW 10: Purl.
ROW 11: Knit.
ROW 12: Purl.
ROWS 13–24: As rows 11–12, ending with a WS row.
ROW 25–82: Work as for Back.
Bind (cast) off.

Twisted cord

Cut two lengths of yarn A and two lengths of yarn B each approximately 5ft 9in (175cm) long. Take the four lengths of yarn and secure at each end with knots. Ask some one to help you and give them one end of the yarn while you hold the other. With the yarn outstretched, each end needs to be twisted in opposite directions until it shows signs of twisting back on itself. Bring the two ends of the cord together and hold tightly, allowing the two halves to twist together. Smooth out any bumps by running your fingers up and down the cord. You will now have a twisted cord approximately 2ft 4in (70cm) long.

FINISHING

Sew in all the ends.

Using mattress stitch, join the Front and Back by working down one side, across the bottom and up the other side.

Thread twisted cord through the eyelets, starting and finishing at the left-hand side of the bag. Pull together.

CHART

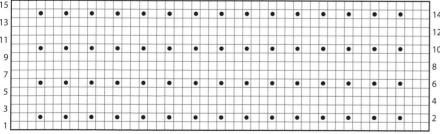

Key

☐   marine (A)

⊡   Place sequin as follows: yf, sl sequin to front of work, sl 1 st purlwise, take yarn to back of work. Sequin will now be sitting in front of slipped st

Clementine

This stylish clutch bag maximizes the luxurious yarn by using double thickness and seed (moss) stitch to create a bold knit. The contrast of the embroidery is accentuated through the use of cotton and lurex, which in turn are highlighted by the glint of the beads.

SIZE
10¾in x 6¾in (27cm x 17cm)

MATERIALS
1 pair US 10 (6mm/no.4) needles

Yarn
Rowan Kid Classic
1¾oz (50g) balls
    juicy (A)   2
    (used double throughout)

Rowan Handknit DK Cotton
    flame   small amount

Rowan Lurex Shimmer
    copper   small amount

Beads
Jaeger
    bronze   approx. 25

GAUGE (TENSION)
15 sts and 24 rows to 4in (10cm) measured over pattern using US 10 (6mm/no.4) needles.

ABBREVIATIONS
beg	beginning
k	knit
p	purl
rem	remaining
RS	right side
st st	stockinette (stocking) stitch
sts	stitches
WS	wrong side

TECHNIQUES
Adding embroidery to knitting, see page 124
Sewing up, see page 125

TIP
When binding (casting) off and then casting on again on the next row to make the handle, it is like making a big buttonhole. To avoid the annoying loop that you can sometimes get in the corner of a buttonhole, on row 34, when you have to cast on 17 sts in between the 16th and the 17th cast-on sts, bring the yarn to the front so it is trapped between the two.

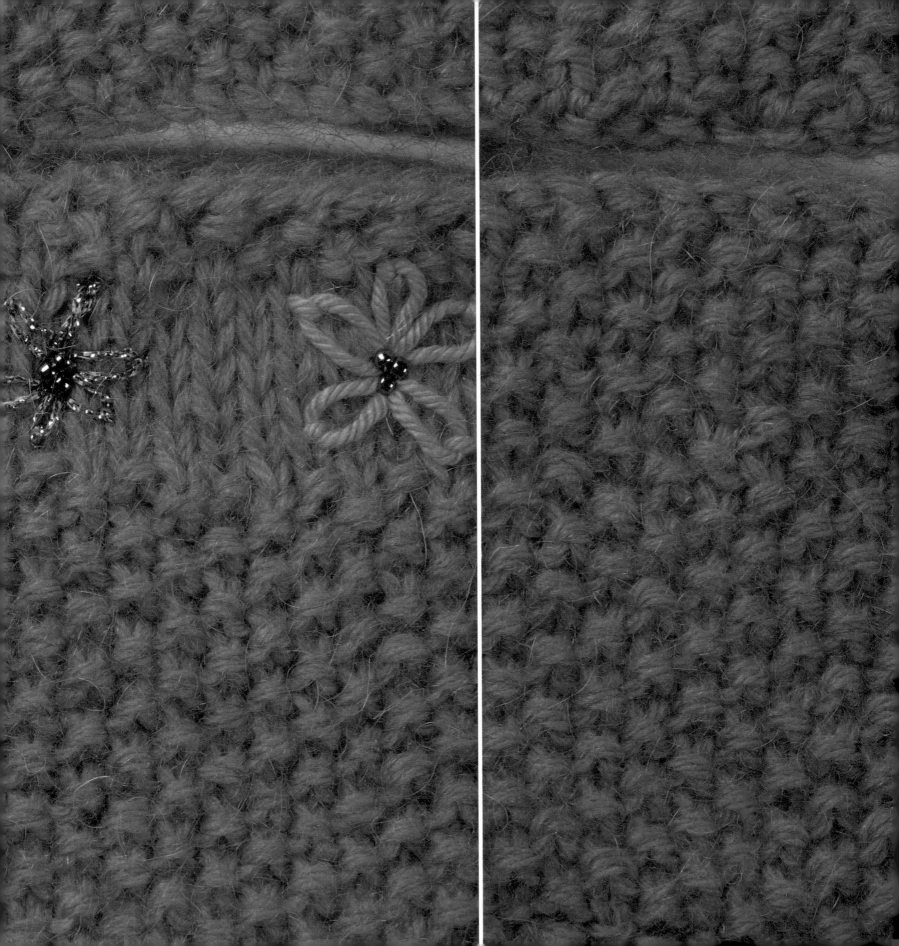

KNIT
Front and Back alike
Using US 10 (6mm/no.4) needles and yarn A, cast on 41 sts.
ROW 1: K1, *p1, k1, rep from * to end.
This row forms seed (moss) stitch.
ROWS 2–24: Rep row 1 twenty-three more times, ending with a WS row.
ROW 25: Knit.
ROW 26: Purl.

ROWS 27–30: Rep last two rows twice more, ending with a WS row.
ROWS 31–32: Rep row 1 twice more, ending with a WS row.
ROW 33 (CREATES HANDLE): seed (moss) st 12 sts, bind (cast) off center 17 sts in pattern, seed (moss) st to end.
ROW 34: seed (moss) st 12 sts, turn, cast on center 17 sts (see Tip), turn, seed (moss) st to end.

ROWS 35–38: Rep row 1 four more times, ending with a WS row.
Bind (cast) off in pattern.

FINISHING
Sew in all the ends.
    Using the daisy stitch as described on page 124, embroider five flowers (three using Handknit Cotton and two using Lurex Shimmer alternated as in

photograph) along the st st border, just below the handle on the front of the bag.
    Using a suitable sewing cotton, stitch a small cluster of beads in the center of each flower.
    Using mattress stitch, join the Front and Back by working down one side, across the bottom and up the other side.

Vamp

This opulent mixture of deep wine red and metallic gold and copper makes an indulgent evening bag with a quirky shape. The subtle choice of colors for the heart intarsia panel only hints at the textural delights. Further interest is added by the layering of twisted cords to create the handle.

SIZE
8½in x 7in (22cm x 18cm)

MATERIALS
1 pair US 7 (4.5mm/no.7) needles

Yarn
Rowan Kid Classic
1¾oz (50g) balls
   crushed velvet (A)   1

Rowan Lurex Shimmer
1oz (25g) balls
   claret (B)   1
   copper (C)   1
   (used double throughout)

GAUGE (TENSION)
20 sts and 24 rows to 4in (10cm) measured over stockinette (stocking) stitch using US 7 (4.5mm/no.7) needles.

ABBREVIATIONS
beg   beginning
dec   decrease
k   knit
p   purl
rem   remaining
RS   right side
st st   stockinette (stocking)
        stitch
sts   stitches
WS   wrong side

TECHNIQUES
Intarsia, see page 118
Sewing in ends, see page 118
Sewing up, see page 125

KNIT
Front
Using US 7 (4.5mm/no.7) needles and yarn A, cast on 45 sts.
ROW 1: **K1, *p1, k1, rep from * to end.**
This row forms seed (moss) stitch.
ROWS 2–16: **Rep row 1 fifteen more times, ending with a WS row.**
ROWS 17–33: **Using the intarsia method described on page 118, work 17 rows from chart in st st, beg with a k (RS) row and ending with purl (WS) row.**
Change to yarn A.
ROW 34: **Purl.**
ROW 35: **K2tog, k to last 2 sts, k2tog. (43 sts)**
ROW 36: **P2tog, p to last 2 sts, p2tog. (41 sts)**
ROWS 37–44: **Rep rows 35 and 36 until 25 sts.**

ROW 45: **Rep row 35 again. (23 sts)**
Change to yarn B.
ROW 46: **Purl.**
Change to yarn A.
ROWS 47–53: **As row 1, ending with a RS row.**
ROW 54: **Knit (this creates garter st ridge for turn over at top of bag).**
Change to yarn C.
ROW 55: **Knit.**
ROW 56: **Purl.**
ROWS 57–60: **Rep last 2 rows, ending with a WS row.**
Bind (cast) off.

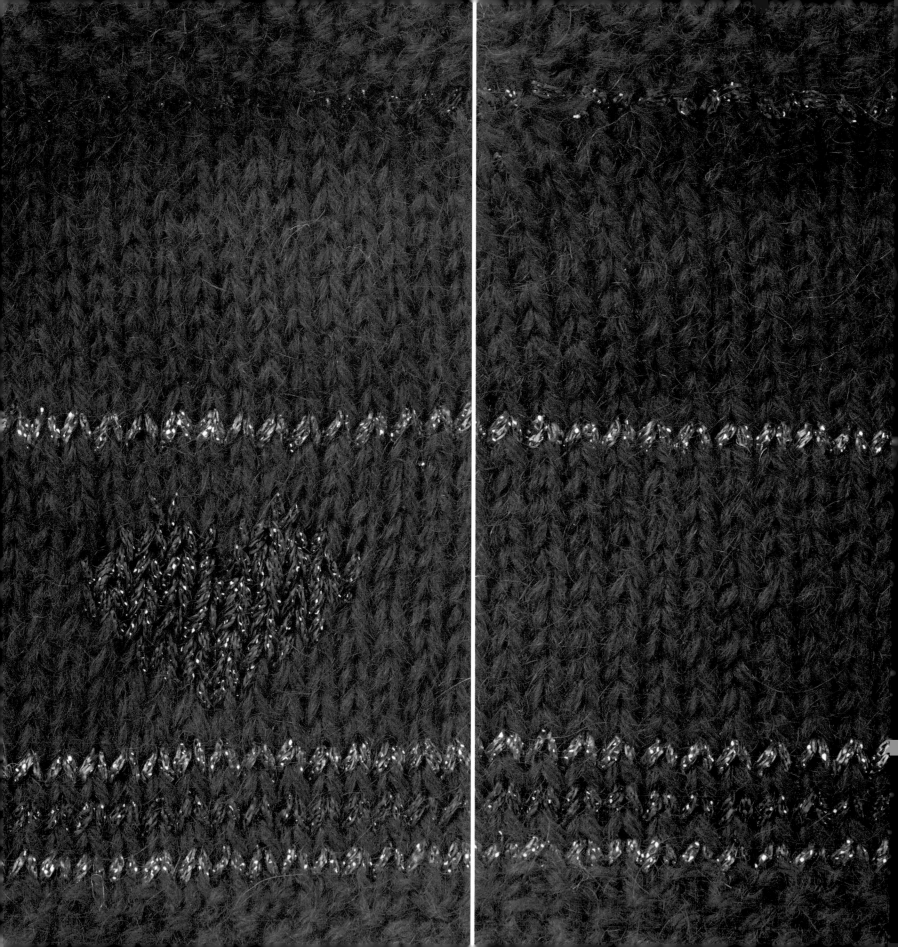

CHART

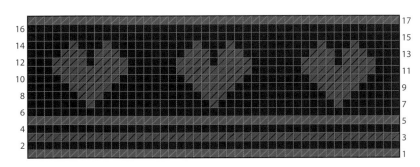

Key

■ crushed velvet (A)
▨ claret (B)
▧ copper (C)

Back

Using US 7 (4.5mm/no.7) needles and yarn A, cast on 45 sts.
ROW 1–16: **Work as for Front.**
ROWS 17–21: **Work rows 1–5 from chart.**
ROW 22: **Purl.**
ROW 23: **Knit.**
ROW 24: **Purl.**
ROWS 25–32: **As rows 23–24.**
ROW 33: **Row 17 from the chart, ending with a RS row.**
Change to yarn A.
ROW 34: **Purl.**
ROW 35: **K2tog, k to last 2 sts, k2tog. (43 sts)**
ROW 36: **P2tog, p to last 2 sts, p2tog. (41 sts)**
ROWS 37–44: **Rep rows 35 and 36 until 25 sts.**
ROW 45: **Rep row 35 again. (23 sts)**
Change to yarn B.
ROW 46: **Purl.**

Change to yarn A.
ROWS 47–53: **As row 1, ending with a RS row.**
ROW 54: **Knit (this creates garter st ridge for turn over at top of bag).**
Change to yarn C.
ROW 55: **Knit.**
ROW 56: **Purl.**
ROWS 57–60: **Rep last 2 rows, ending with a WS row.**
Bind (cast) off.

Twisted cord (make 3)

Cut two lengths of yarn A and two lengths of yarn B each approximately 2ft 3in (68cm) long. Take the four lengths of yarn and secure at each end with knots. Ask some one to help you and give them one end of the yarn while you hold the other. With the yarn outstretched, each end needs to be twisted in opposite directions until it shows signs of twisting back on itself. Bring the two ends of the cord together and hold tightly, allowing the two halves to twist together. Smooth out any bumps by running your fingers up and down the cord. You will now have a twisted cord approximately 10½in (27cm) long.

FINISHING

Sew in all the ends.
   Using mattress stitch, join the Front and Back by working down one side, across the bottom and up the other side.
   Fold down the turn over at the top of the bag along the garter st ridge and, using yarn A, slip stitch into place.
   Tie the three twisted cords together with a knot at each end and then sew neatly and securely at the top of the bag inside the side seams.

Jet

Cotton and mohair are worked together to make a very dense, tactile knit. The delicate flower uses only mohair to provide relief against the heavy body of the bag. The evening feel is finished off with a scattering of beads in the center of the flower.

SIZE
7½in x 7in (19cm x 18cm), excluding handle

MATERIALS
1 pair US 10 (6mm/no.4) needles
1 pair US 3 (3.25mm/no.10) needles

Yarn
Rowan Cotton Glacé
1¾oz (50g) balls
    mystic (A)   2
    (used double throughout)

Rowan Kid Silk Haze
1oz (25g) balls
    smoke (B)   1
    (used double throughout)

Beads
Jaeger
    gray   approx. 20

GAUGE (TENSION)
14 sts and 19 rows to 4in (10cm) measured over pattern using US 10 (6mm/no.4) needles.

ABBREVIATIONS
beg	beginning
k	knit
p	purl
rem	remaining
rep	repeat
RS	right side
st st	stockinette (stocking) stitch
sts	stitches
WS	wrong side

TECHNIQUES
Sewing in ends, see page 118
Sewing up, see page 125

KNIT

Front and Back alike

Using US 10 (6mm/no.4) needles and 2 strands of yarn A and 2 strands of yarn B, cast on 27 sts.

ROW 1: Knit.

ROW 2: K1, *p1, k1, rep from * to end.

ROWS 3–28: Rep rows 1 and 2 thirteen more times, ending with a WS row.

ROW 29 (RS): Knit.

ROW 30 (WS): Purl.

These last two rows form st st.

ROWS 31–36: Rep rows 29 and 30 three times, ending with a WS row.

ROW 37 (RS): As row 29.

ROWS 38–39: Rep row 29 twice more (this creates garter st ridge for turn over at top of bag).

ROW 40: As row 30.

ROWS 41–42: Rep rows 29 and 30 once more, ending with a WS row. Bind (cast) off.

Handle (make 1)

Using US 10 (6mm/no.4) needles, cast on 5 sts.

ROW 1: Knit.

ROW 2: K1, p3, k1.

Rep last 2 rows until handle measures 10in (25cm), ending with a WS row.

Bind (cast) off.

Flower

Using US 3 (3.25mm/no.10) needles and one strand of yarn B, cast on 193 sts

ROW 1: K1, *k2, lift first of these 2 over second, rep from * to end.

ROW 2: (P2tog) to last st, p1. (49 sts)

Change to yarn A.

ROW 3: Knit.

ROW 4: Purl.

ROW 5: K1, (k2tog) to end. (25 sts)

Break off yarn, thread through rem stitches and pull together. Twist ruffle round into a flower shape and secure using yarn still attached.

FINISHING

Sew in all the ends.

Using mattress stitch, join the Front and Back by working down one side, across the bottom and up the other side.

Fold down the turn over at the top of the bag along the garter st ridge and slip stitch into place. Do this for the Front and the Back.

Sew flower neatly and securely into place at top left of bag, as in photograph.

Using a suitable sewing cotton, stitch a small cluster of beads in the center of the flower.

Slip stitch handle securely in place inside the side seams at top of the bag.

Heather

This is an intricate bag that uses a textural combination of beads, cable, and crochet, to create a subtle range of lilacs, which shimmer alongside each other. This is a very feminine and elegant bag, perfect for a dazzling night out.

SIZE
6½in x 6½in (17cm x 17cm), excluding handle

MATERIALS
1 pair US 7 (4.5mm/no.7) needles
1 cable needle
1 D/3 (3mm) crochet hook

Yarn
Rowan Calmer
1¾oz (50g) balls
   chiffon (A)   2

Rowan Lurex
1¾oz (50g) balls
   gleam (B)   1

Beads
   pale pink   approx. 84

GAUGE (TENSION)
29 sts and 34 rows to 4in (10cm) measured over cable pattern using US 7 (4.5mm/no.7) needles.

ABBREVIATIONS
beg	beginning
c4b	cable 4 back: slip next 3 sts onto a cable needle and hold at back of work, k2, then k2 from the cable needle
dc	single crochet in UK
k	knit
p	purl
pb	place bead: yarn forward, slip bead to front of work, slip 1 st purlwise, take yarn to back of work. Bead will now be sitting in front of the slipped stitch
rem	remaining
RS	right side
sc	single crochet in US
st st	stockinette (stocking) stitch
sts	stitches
WS	wrong side

TECHNIQUES
Cables, see page 123
Knitting with beads, see page 120
Sewing up, see page 125

KNIT

Front

Using US 7 (4.5mm/no.7) needles and yarn A, cast on 52 sts.

ROW 1: **K1, *p1, k3, p1, k4, rep from * to last 6 sts, p1, k3, p1, k1.**

ROW 2: **K2, *p3, k1, p4, k1, rep from * to last 5 sts, p3, k2.**

ROW 3: **K1, *p1, k1, pb, k1, p1, k4, rep from * to last 6 sts, p1, k1, pb, k1, p1, k1.**

ROW 4: **As row 2.**

ROW 5: **K1, *p1, k3, p1, C4B, rep from * to last 6 sts, p1, k3, p1, k1.**

ROW 6: **As row 2.**

ROWS 7–58: **Rep rows 3–6 thirteen more times, ending with a WS row. Bind (cast) off in pattern.**

Back

Using US 7 (4.5mm/no.7) needles and yarn A, cast on 52 sts.

ROW 1: **K1, *p1, k3, p1, k4, rep from * to last 6 sts, p1, k3, p1, k1.**

ROW 2: **K2, *p3, k1, p4, k1, rep from * to last 5 sts, p3, k2.**

ROWS 3–58: **Rep rows 1 and 2 twenty-eight more times, ending with a WS row. Bind (cast) off in pattern.**

Handle (make 1)

Using US 7 (4.5mm/no.7) needles and yarn A, cast on 5 sts.

ROW 1: **Knit.**

ROW 2: **K1, p3, k1.**

Rep last 2 rows until handle measures 9in (23cm), ending with a WS row.
Bind (cast) off.

Edging

Using D/3 (3mm) crochet hook and yarn B, work crochet edging as follows:
Slip st into first bound (cast) off st,* work 5sc (dc) into next st, slip st into next st, miss 2 sts, rep from * to last 3 sts, work 5sc (dc) into next st, miss 1 st, slip st into last bound (cast) off st.

FINISHING

Sew in all the ends.

Using mattress stitch, join the Front and Back by working down one side, across the bottom and up the other side.

Slip stitch handle securely in place inside the side seams at top of the bag.

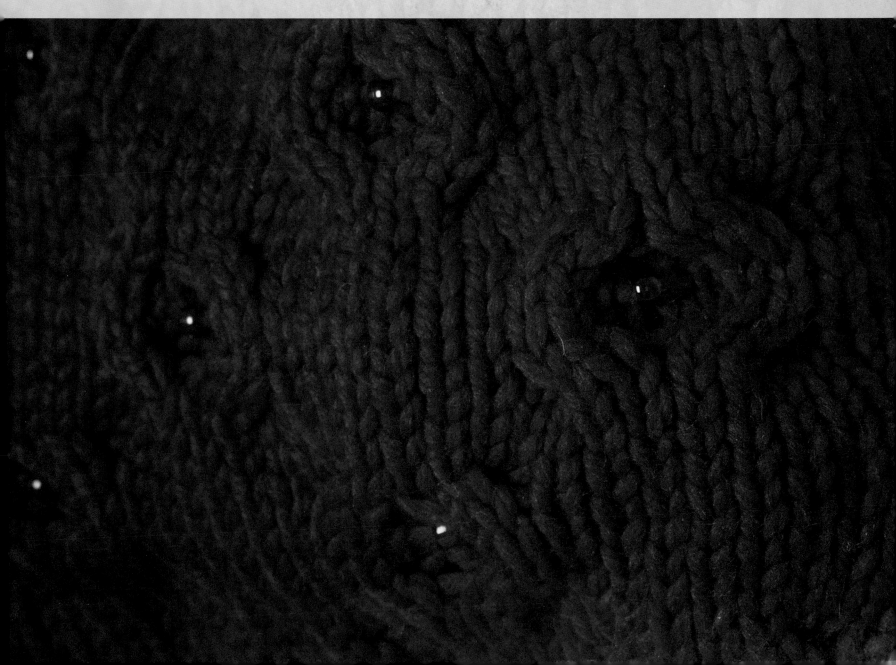

Chunky bags

Arctic

This bag is very thick thanks to a combination of seed (moss) stitch and an alpaca mix, which create a very dense and sumptuous fabric. The flowers are also knitted and are used to create a striking relief against the bag itself.

SIZE
13½in x 11½in (34cm x 29cm), excluding handle

MATERIALS
1 pair US 10½ (7mm/no.2) needles

Yarn
Rowan Polar
3½oz (100g) balls
    the blues (A)   2
    silver lining (B)   1

GAUGE (TENSION)
13 sts and 20 rows to 4in (10cm) measured over pattern using US 10½ (7mm/no.2) needles.

ABBREVIATIONS
beg	beginning
k	knit
p	purl
rem	remaining
RS	right side
sts	stitches
WS	wrong side

TECHNIQUES
Sewing in ends, see page 118
Sewing up, see page 125

KNIT
Front and Back alike
Using US 10½ (7mm/no.2) needles and yarn A, cast on 45 sts.
ROW 1: K1, *p1, k1, rep from * to end.
This row forms seed (moss) stitch.
ROWS 2–58: As row 1, ending with a WS row.
Change to yarn B.
ROWS 59–60: Knit (this creates a garter st ridge for turn over at top of bag).

Change to yarn A.
ROW 61: Knit.
ROW 62: Purl.
ROWS 63–70: Rep last 2 rows four more times, ending with a WS row.
Bind (cast) off.

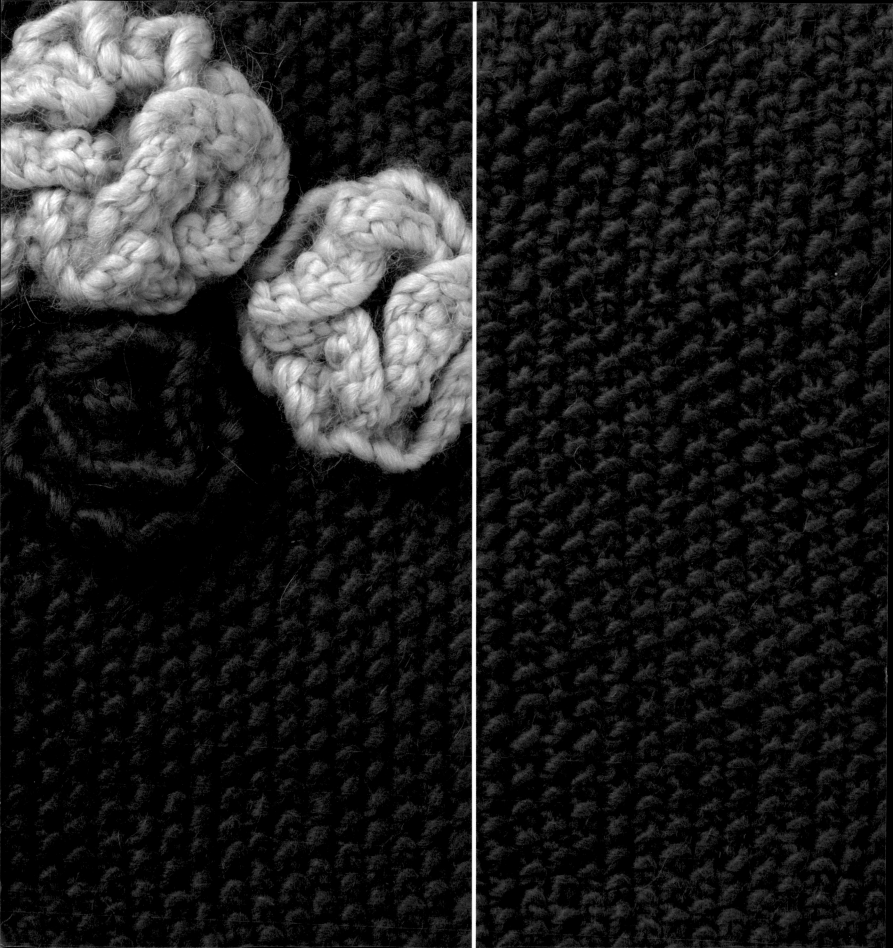

Handles (make 2)
Using US 10½ (7mm/no.2) needles and yarn A, cast on 7 sts.
ROW 1: Knit.
ROW 2: K1, p5, k1.
Rep last 2 rows until handle measures 17¾in (45cm), ending with a WS row.
Bind (cast) off in pattern.

Flowers
Large flower
Using US 10½ (7mm/no.2) needles and yarn B, cast on 161 sts.
ROW 1: K1, *k2, lift first of these 2 over second, rep from * to end.
ROW 2: (P2tog) to last st, p1. (41 sts)
Change to yarn A.
ROW 3: (K2tog) to last st, k1. (21 sts)
Change to yarn B.
ROW 4: P1, (p2tog) to end. (11 sts)
Break off yarn, thread through rem stitches and pull together. Twist ruffle into flower shape and secure using yarn still attached.

1st small flower
Using US 10½ (7mm/no.2) needles and yarn A, cast on 73 sts.
ROW 1: K1, *k2, lift first of these 2 over second, rep from * to end.
ROW 2: (P2tog) to last st, p1. (19 sts)
Change to yarn B.
ROW 3: (K2tog) to last st, k1. (10 sts)
Break off yarn, thread through rem stitches and pull together. Twist ruffle into flower shape and secure using yarn still attached.

2nd small flower
Work as for first small flower replacing yarn A with B and yarn B with A.

FINISHING
Sew in all the ends.

Using mattress stitch, join together the Front and Back by working down one side, across the bottom and up the other side.

Fold down the turn over at the top of the bag along the garter st ridge and, using yarn A, slip stitch into place. Do this for both the Front and the Back.

Sew flowers neatly and securely into place at top left of bag, as in photograph.

Slip stitch handles securely in place approximately 2¾in (7cm) in from the side seams. Do this for the Front and Back.

Sherbet

This bag is a lot of fun and very tactile. The large pompoms act as a drawstring for the bag, which also uses a chunky yarn to maximum effect. You could cram a lot of things in this bag, although it's practically bursting with energy already!

SIZE
15¾in x 12in (40cm x 30cm), excluding handle

MATERIALS
1 pair US 11 (7.5mm/no.1) needles

Yarn
Rowan Chunky Print
3½oz (100g) balls
  girly pink (A)   2
  silver lining (B)   1

GAUGE (TENSION)
12 sts and 16 rows to 4in (10cm) measured over pattern using US 11 (7.5mm/no.1) needles.

ABBREVIATIONS
beg	beginning
inc	increase
k	knit
m1	make one stitch
p	purl
rem	remaining
rep	repeat
RS	right side
st st	stockinette (stocking) stitch
sts	stitches
tog	together
WS	wrong side
yf	yarn forward

TECHNIQUES
Sewing in ends, see page 118
Sewing up, see page 125

KNIT
Front and Back alike
Using US 11 (7.5mm/no.1) needles and yarn B, cast on 161 sts.
ROW 1: **K1, *k2, lift first of these 2 over second, rep from * to end.**
ROW 2: **(p2tog) to last st, p1. (41 sts)**
Change to yarn A.
ROW 3 (RS): **Knit.**
ROW 4 (WS): **Purl.**
These two rows form st st.
ROWS 5–8: **Rep rows 3 and 4 twice more, ending with a WS row.**
ROW 9 (RS): **K2, yf, k2tog, *k3, yf, k2tog, rep from * to last 2 sts, k2.**
ROW 10: **As row 4.**
ROWS 11–14: **Rep rows 3 and 4 twice more, ending with a WS row.**
ROW 15 (INC ROW): **K1, m1, k to last st, m1, k1. (43 sts)**
ROW 16: **As row 4.**

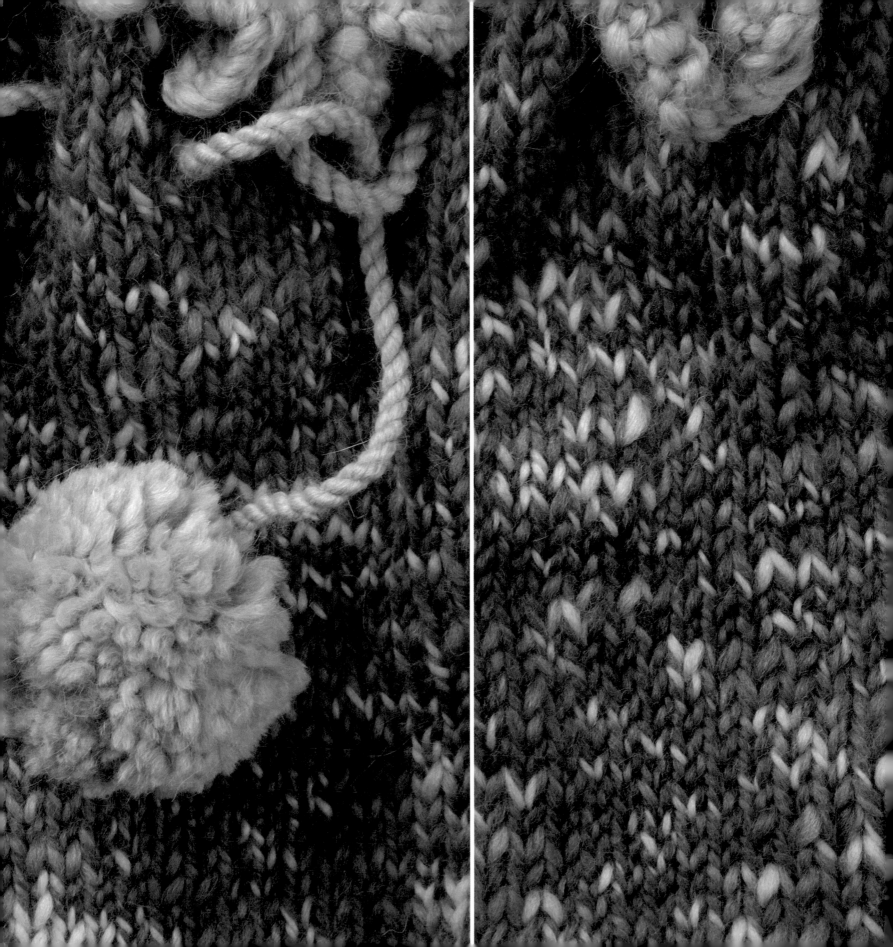

ROWS 17–18: **Rep rows 3 and 4.**

ROW 19: **As row 15. (45 sts)**

ROWS 20–31: **Rep rows 16 to 19 three more times, ending with a RS row. (51 sts)**

ROW 32: **As row 4.**

ROWS 33–36: **Rep rows 3 and 4 twice more, ending with a WS row.**

ROW 37: **As row 15. (53 sts)**

ROW 38: **As row 4.**

ROWS 39–48: **Rep rows 3 and 4 five more times, ending with a WS row. Bind (cast) off.**

Handle (make 1)

Using US 11 (7.5mm/no.1) needles and yarn B, cast on 7 sts.

ROW 1: **Knit.**

ROW 2: **K1, p5, k1.**

Rep last 2 rows until handle measures 17½in (44cm).

Twisted cord

Cut three lengths of yarn B approximately 4ft 1in (125cm) long. Take the three lengths of yarn and secure at each end with knots. Ask some one to help you and give them one end of the yarn while you hold the other. With the yarn outstretched, each end needs to be twisted in opposite directions until it shows signs of twisting back on itself. Bring the two ends of the cord together and hold tightly, allowing the two halves to twist together. Smooth out any bumps by running your fingers up and down the cord. You will now have a twisted cord approximately 20in (50cm) long.

Pompoms (make 2)

Cut two circles of card approximately 2½in (6cm) in diameter. Cut a hole in the center of each approximately 1¼in (3cm) in diameter. Using yarn B, wind the yarn around the outside of the two circles of card until the hole in the center is almost filled in. Next, cut slowly and carefully round the edges of the two pieces of card until all the yarn has been cut. Carefully ease the pieces of card apart but BEFORE taking them off completely, tie a piece of yarn in a secure knot around the center of the pompom to hold it together. Now remove the card.

FINISHING

Sew in all the ends.

Using mattress stitch, join the Front and Back by working down one side, across the bottom and up the other side.

Slip stitch handles securely in place approximately ¾in (2cm) in from the side seams. Do this for the Front and Back.

Thread the twisted cord through the eyelets starting and finishing at the middle of the front.

Sew pompoms to each end of the twisted cord neatly and securely.

Cranberry

This is a chunky, textured bag that uses the thick yarn to exaggerate the cabling technique. Beads are used to add even more texture to the twists and turns as they work their way up the bag. With cables and beading, this is just the bag to show off all of your handiwork.

SIZE
14¼in x 11¼in (36cm x 30cm), excluding handle

MATERIALS
1 pair US 15 (10mm/no.000) needles

Yarn
Rowan Big Wool
3½oz (100g) balls
  cassis   2

Beads
  dark red   approx. 20

GAUGE (TENSION)
11 sts and 13 rows to 4in (10cm) measured over cable pattern using US 15 (10mm/no.000) needles.

ABBREVIATIONS
beg   beginning
c4b   cable 4 back: slip next 2 sts onto a cable needle and hold at back of work, k2, then k2 from the cable needle
c4f   cable 4 front: slip next 2 sts onto a cable needle and hold at front of work, k2, then k2 from the cable needle
k   knit
p   purl
pb   place bead: yarn forward, slip bead to front of work, slip 2 sts purlwise, take yarn to back of work. Bead will now be sitting in front of the 2 slipped stitches
rem   remaining
RS   right side
st st   stockinette (stocking) stitch
sts   stitches
WS   wrong side

TECHNIQUES
Cables, see page 123
Knitting with beads, see page 120
Sewing in ends, see page 118
Sewing up, see page 125

KNIT
Front
Using US 15 (10mm/no.000) needles, cast on 42 sts.
ROW 1: Knit.
ROW 2: Purl.
ROW 3: K3, *c4b, c4f, k6, rep from * to last 11 sts, c4b, c4f, k3.
ROW 4: Purl.
ROW 5: K6, pb, k12, pb, k12, pb, k6.
ROW 6: Purl.
ROW 7: K3, *c4f, c4b, k6, rep from * to last 11 sts, c4f, c4b, k3.
ROW 8: Purl.
ROW 9: Knit.

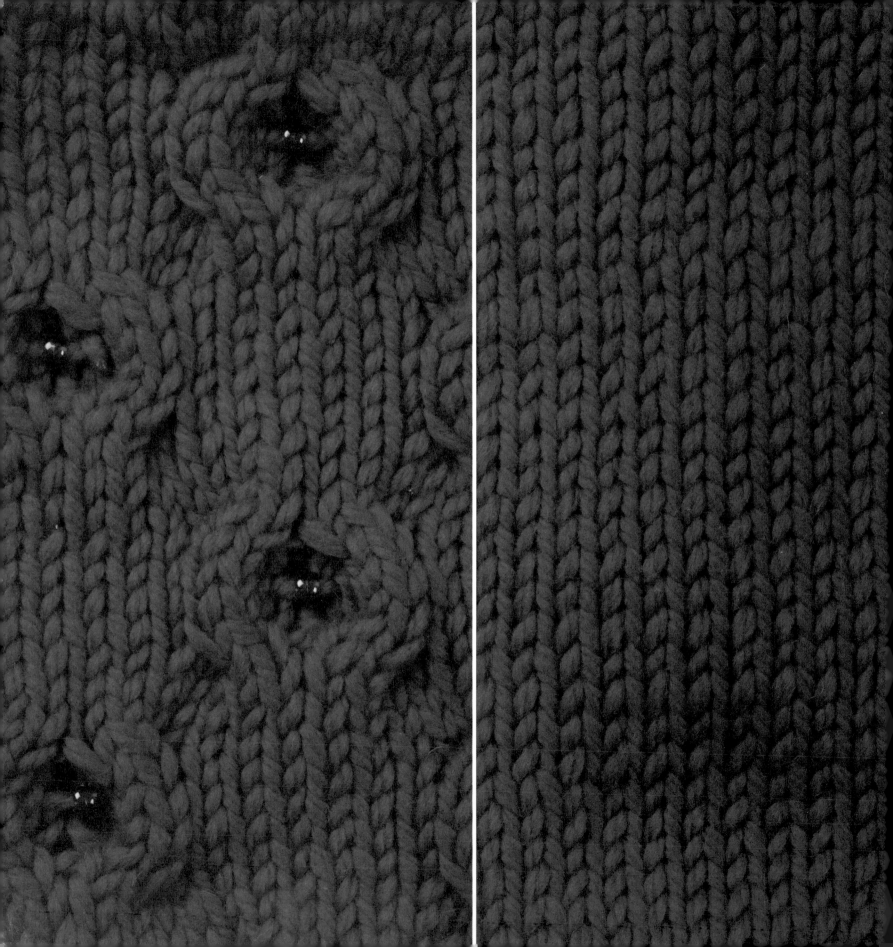

ROW 10: **Purl.**
ROW 11: **K10, c4b, c4f, k6, c4b, c4f, k10.**
ROW 12: **Purl.**
ROW 13: **K13, pb, k12, pb, k13.**
ROW 14: **Purl.**
ROW 15: **K10, c4f, c4b, k6, c4f, c4b, k10.**
ROW 16: **Purl.**
ROW 17: **Knit.**
ROW 18: **Purl.**
Rep rows 3–18 once more, then rows 3–9 again, ending with a RS row.
ROW 42: **Knit (this creates a garter st ridge for turn over at top of bag).**
ROW 43: **Knit.**
ROW 44: **Purl.**
ROWS 45–46: **Rep rows 43–44, ending with a WS row.**
Bind (cast) off.

Back
Using US 15 (10mm/no.000) needles, cast on 34 sts.
ROW 1: **Knit.**
ROW 2: **Purl.**
Rep last 2 rows until 41 rows have been worked ending with a RS row.
ROW 42: **Knit (this creates a garter st ridge for turn over at top of bag).**
ROW 43: **Knit.**
ROW 44: **Purl.**
ROWS 45–46: **Rep last 2 rows, ending with a WS row.**
Bind (cast) off.

Handles (make 2)
Using US 15 (10mm/no.000) needles and yarn A, cast on 5 sts.
ROW 1: **Knit.**
ROW 2: **K1, p3, k1.**
Rep last 2 rows until handle measures 17½in (44cm), ending with a WS row.
Bind (cast) off.

FINISHING
Sew in all the ends.

Using mattress stitch, join the Front and Back by working down one side, across the bottom and up the other side.

Fold down the turn over at the top of the bag along the garter st ridge and, using yarn A, slip stitch into place. Do this for the Front and the Back.

Slip stitch handles securely in place approximately 4½in (11cm) in from the side seams. Do this for the Front and Back.

Techniques

INTARSIA KNITTING

Intarsia knitting produces a single thickness fabric that uses different balls of yarn for different areas of color. There should be very little, if any, carrying across of yarns at the back of the work.

There are several ways to help keep the separate colors of yarn organized while you are working. My preferred method is to use yarn bobbins. Small amounts of yarn can be wound onto bobbins, which should then be kept close to the back of the work while knitting, and only unwound when more yarn is needed.

The intarsia patterns in this book are given in the form of a chart. It is advisable to make a color copy of the chart and to enlarge it if you prefer. This copy can be used as a worksheet on which rows can be marked off as they are worked and any notes can be made.

Joining in a new color

1 Insert the right needle into the next stitch. Place the end of the new pink yarn between the tips of the needles and across the purple yarn from left to right.

2 Take the new pink yarn under the purple yarn and knit the next stitch with it. Carefully move the tail of pink yarn off the right needle as the new stitch is formed.

Changing colors

To avoid gaps between stitches when changing color, it is essential that the two yarns are crossed over at the back of the work.

1 On a knit row, insert the right needle into the next stitch. Place the old purple yarn over the new pink yarn. Pull the new pink yarn up and knit the stitch.

2 On a purl row, insert the right needle into the next stitch. Place the old pink yarn over the new purple yarn. Pull the new purple yarn up and purl the next stitch.

Sewing in ends

When an intarsia area is completed there will be loose ends to darn in on the back of the work.

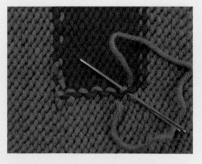 

1 Darn the ends around shapes by darning through the loops of the same color in one direction first.

2 Then darn the end back on itself, stretching the work before cutting the end of the yarn.

FAIR ISLE KNITTING

Stranding is used when the yarn not in use is left at the back of the work until needed. The loops formed by stranding are called "floats" and it is important to ensure that they are not pulled too tightly when working the next stitch as this will pull in your knitting. If the gap between the colors is more than four stitches, the weaving-in method (described below) is preferable as this prevents too long floats that stop the fabric having the right amount of elasticity. Many color patterns will use both techniques and you will choose the one that is the most appropriate to a particular part of the design.

Stranding

1   On a knit row, hold the first color in your right hand and the second color in your left hand. Knit the required number of stitches as usual with the first color, carrying the second color loosely across the wrong side of the work.

2   To knit a stitch in the second color, insert the right-hand needle into the next stitch then draw a loop through from the yarn held in the left hand, carrying the yarn in the right hand loosely across the wrong side until required.

3   On a purl row, hold the yarns as for the knit rows. Purl the required number of stitches as usual with the first color, carrying the second color loosely across these stitches on the wrong side of the work.

4   To purl a stitch in the second color, insert the right-hand needle into the next stitch then draw a loop through from the yarn held in the left hand, carrying the yarn in the right hand loosely across the wrong side until next required.

Weaving

Weaving in, or knitting in, the floats are caught in by the working yarn on every alternate stitch, or preferably on every third or fourth stitch. (Weaving in on every alternate stitch can distort the stitches and alter the gauge.) Insert the right-hand needle into the stitch. Lay the contrast yarn over the point of the right-hand needle then knit the stitch in the usual way, taking care not to knit in the contrast yarn. When you knit the next stitch, the contrast yarn will have been caught in. Use the same method to catch in the yarn on the purl rows.

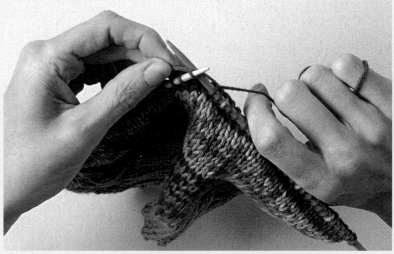

1   On a knit row, hold the first color in your right hand and the second color in your left hand. Knit the required number of rows.

Fancy Yarns

Color knitting offers a wonderful opportunity to incorporate fancy yarns into garments. Gold and silver lurex yarns tend to look garish on their own, but can add subtle sparkle and a touch of glamor to knitwear when used in small quantities. Try working lurex into a Fair Isle pattern to give a new touch to a traditional design. Mohair and angora yarns can work well too. Do experiment with combining different types of yarn; the results can be wonderful.

KNITTING WITH BEADS

There are many different types of beads available, but not all of them are suitable for hand-knitting. When choosing beads it is important to check that the bead hole is big enough for the yarn to pass through. In addition, the weight and size of the beads also needs to be considered. For example, large heavy beads on 4-ply knitting will look clumsy and cause the fabric to sag. It is also wise to check whether the beads you are using are washable, as some may not be.

When you have chosen your beads, you must thread them onto the yarn before you start to knit. There is a very easy way to do this.

Threading beads onto yarn

Place a length of sewing cotton beneath the yarn, then bring the two ends of the cotton together and thread both ends through a sewing needle. Thread the beads onto the needle, then push them down the sewing cotton and onto the knitting yarn. Remember that the first bead you thread onto the yarn will be the last one to be knitted in.

ADDING BEADS WITH A SLIP STITCH

This is my preferred method of adding beads to knitting, and it works on both wrong-side and right-side rows. The beads sit in front of a slipped stitch and hang down slightly from where they are knitted in. I have found that if the yarn is held quite firmly and the next stitch after the bead is knitted tightly, the bead sits very neatly and snugly against the knitting.

Adding beads on a right side row

1 Work to where the bead is to be placed. Bring the yarn forward between the points of the needles.

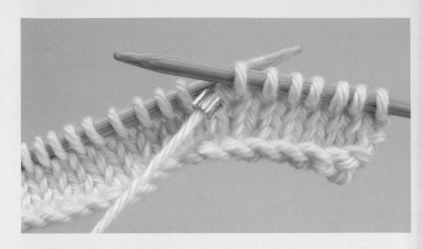

2 Push a bead up the yarn to the front of the work, so that it rests in front of the right-hand needle.

3 Slip the next stitch purlwise from the left-hand to the right-hand needle, leaving the bead in front of the slipped stitch.

4 Take the yarn between the needles to the back of the work and continue in pattern. The bead is now secured in position.

Adding beads on a wrong side row

When beads are placed on a wrong side row, the instructions are almost the same.

1 When a bead is to be added, take the yarn back between the needle points and push a bead up to the front of the work.

2 Slip the next stitch exactly as above.

3 Bring the yarn forward and continue working. On the next row work the slip stitch firmly.

Adding beads to reverse stockinette (stocking) stitch

The principle is the same. Place the bead with the yarn at front of work. Slide a bead up so that it rests in front of the right-hand needle. Slip the next stitch purlwise and keeping yarn at front of work pull firmly so that bead sits in front of slipped stitch then purl the next stitch.

KNITTING WITH SEQUINS

Some sequins are plain in color, but there are also some sequins that resemble mini-holograms, and these create quite spectacular multi-colored effects when held in the light. Sequins not only add extra color and sparkle to a knitted fabric, but they also change the quality and feel of the knitting.

When choosing sequins it is important to remember that the hole through the center must be big enough for the yarn to pass through. The size of the sequin should also be considered, and chosen in relation to the weight of yarn used. And, as with beads, it is also best to check if the sequins are washable before buying them.

The method of adding sequins to knitting is identical to the way that beads are knitted in. However, care should be taken to hold the sequins flat to the fabric while knitting, ensuring that they are all laying the same way. And it is advisable only to place sequins while working on a right side row, as it is extremely difficult to do this on a wrong side row.

CABLES

Cables are the crossing of one set of stitches over another to create a twisted rope effect. Stitches can be crossed over at the front or the back of the work; this determines whether the cable twists to the left or to the right. Stitches held at the front of the work will twist the cable to the left, stitches held at the back of the work will twist the cable to the right. Cables are usually knitted in stockinette (stocking) stitch on a background of reverse stockinette (stocking) stitch, though a background of stockinette (stocking) stitch can also work well. Usually the number of stitches that are crossed are half of the amount stated in the abbreviation, ie: c8b means cross 4 stitches with 4 stitches. There are many different variations, so it is best to read the instructions carefully before starting to knit. This example shows how to work c8b.

c8b

1 Slip the next 4 stitches onto the cable needle and hold at the back of the work.

2 Knit 4 stitches from the left-hand needle.

3 Then knit the 4 stitches that are on the cable needle.

Make sure that you pull the yarn firmly and knit the stitches tightly to avoid any gaps in the work.

ADDING EMBROIDERY TO KNITTING

Outlines, single dots or fancy shapes and textures can be added to your fabric after knitting. It is advisable to finish your knitting and tidy up the loose ends before embroidering. A large, blunt darning needle should be used to avoid splitting the stitches. A yarn of the same or a slightly heavier weight as the main knitting that will easily cover the stitches is recommended.

I have used Swiss darning in various projects in this book. This is a method of duplicating knitted stitches on stockinette (stocking) stitch fabrics using a needle and a separate length of yarn. It is a quick and easy way of adding dashes of color or outlines, and it can be worked horizontally or vertically.

Swiss darning (worked horizontally)

 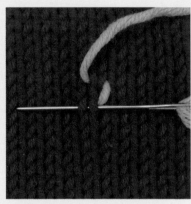

1 From the back of the work, insert the needle through the base of the knitted stitch, then take the needle around the top of the knitted stitch.

2 From the front of the work, insert the needle into the base of the same knitted stitch and out through the base of the next knitted stitch on the left.

3 Pull the yarn through. You have now covered a stitch. Repeat the process until you have completed the work.

Swiss darning (worked vertically)

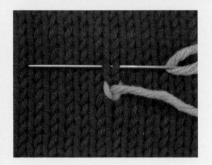

1 Darn the first stitch as for horizontal darning, but bring the needle out through the base of the stitch above the one just worked. Work that stitch in the same way. Continue forming the stitches, but work upwards rather than from right to left.

BLOCKING AND PRESSING

The blocking and pressing of knitting is an essential part of the finishing process, and one that is often omitted by knitters. There are several reasons why blocking and pressing should be done. Firstly, it flattens the edges of the knitting, which makes it easier to pick up stitches or sew together panels. Secondly, it ensures that the panels are the correct size. And lastly, it finishes the knitted fabric, and in most cases changes the physical quality of the knitting, smoothing out stitches and making the fabric feel softer and more fluid.

Blocking is the pinning out of the knitted pieces, which should be done on a flat surface with the wrong side facing up. A tape measure should be used to ensure that the pieces are of the correct size. The temperature of the iron used for pressing is dependant on the fiber content of the yarn, as is the damp or dry pressing cloth, which must completely cover the panel that is going to be pressed. The general rule is as follows: natural fibers require a damp pressing cloth and a warm iron, and synthetic fibers and mixes require a dry pressing cloth and a cool iron. However, not all yarns conform to these rules and some have alternative requirements, so it is always advisable to read the pressing instructions that are printed on the ball band. If several different yarns have been used in one piece of knitting, it is better to play safe and follow the instructions for the most delicate yarn. If the heat of the iron is too hot, it could ruin the knitting permanently, resulting in a limp and lifeless piece of knitting that is irreversible.

After pressing it is best to leave the knitting pinned out for at least half an hour to allow all of the heat and moisture to evaporate. Then, when the pins are removed, the knitting will be flat and ready for sewing up.

SEWING UP

After spending time knitting your bag, it is very important that the sewing together of the panels is done as neatly as possible. I would recommend that you use mattress stitch, because it is easy to learn, very precise and it creates an almost invisible seam. One big advantage of using this stitch over other methods of sewing up is that you work with the right sides of the knitting facing up towards you, which enables you to see exactly how the seam is progressing. Mattress stitch also allows you to accurately match stripes or patterns on the back and front panels of the bag.

A blunt sewing-up needle and a matching yarn should be used to sew together the panels. Lay the pieces of knitting out on a flat surface in the arrangement in which they are to be sewn together.

Mattress stitch seam (sewing stitches to stitches)

1 From the back of the work, insert the needle through the center of the first stitch along one of the edges, leaving a long tail of yarn.

2 From the back of the work, insert the needle between the first and the second stitches along the opposite edge.

3 Continue in this way, zigzagging backwards and forwards from edge to edge, and pulling the stitches up to close the seam. Do not pull too hard or the seam will be too tight.

The mattress seam is invisible on the right side. Continue sewing the whole seam, then secure the ends by darning them in.

Mattress stitch seam (sewing rows to rows)

1 From the front, insert the needle between the first and second stitches on the first row. Take the needle under the next row and bring it through to the front again. Pull the yarn through, leaving a long end.

2 Insert the needle the same way into the other edge that is to be joined, but this time bring the needle out two rows above the point where it goes in.

3 Insert the needle into the first edge again, into the hole that the thread last came out of on that edge. Bring the needle out two rows above that point.

4 Repeat, zigzagging from edge to edge for 2in (5cm). Pull the thread up, holding the seam and long end of the yarn with the left hand.

WASHING AND CARING FOR YOUR BAG

Hand-washing

Your bag should be hand-washed to maintain its quality. Use plenty of lukewarm water and a detergent specially formulated for knitwear. The fabric should be gently squeezed and then rinsed in several changes of water. It is a good idea to get rid of excess water by gently spinning the bag in a washing-machine inside a secure wash-bag, such as a pillowcase, to avoid the fabric stretching. This will also protect any beads or buttons. Lay the bag out flat on a towel after washing, and gently ease back into shape. It should then be left alone until it is completely dry.

Dry-cleaning

You can have your bag dry-cleaned, but check that all of the yarns used can be dry-cleaned. Remember that if beads or buttons have been used, the dry-cleaners may refuse to clean it.

yarn information

CHOOSING THE RIGHT YARN

If you want your knitted bag to look like the picture in the book, I would recommend that you use the yarns that I have specified for each design. A substitute yarn that differs in weight, shade, or fiber content will change the whole look, feel, and size of the finished bag.

QUANTITIES OF YARN AND DYE LOTS

At the beginning of each project the quantities of yarn are given for the bag. If different yarns are used, these quantities will alter. This is because the length of a ball of yarn depends on its weight and fiber content: an aran weight cotton will have a shorter length than an aran weight wool, and a 4-ply cotton will have a longer length than a double-knit cotton. The quantities of yarn can be re-calculated if desired. Buy all the yarn you need to complete the project at the same time, checking the ball bands to ensure that all the balls are from the same dye lot. The color of a specific shade of yarn can vary quite a lot between dye lots and the change will show in the finished project.

GAUGE (TENSION) AND SELECTING CORRECT NEEDLE SIZE

The needle sizes that I have recommended for each design have been chosen to create a firm gauge (tension). This is especially important if you are knitting accessories that are going to be handled, such as bags. If the knitting is too loose, the article will easily become misshapen, and will most likely drop and grow in size. Using a slightly smaller needle than the usual recommended size for the yarn ensures that the knitted fabric retains its shape.

Gauge (tension) can differ quite dramatically between knitters. This is because of the way that the needles and the yarn are held. So if your gauge (tension) does not match that stated in the pattern, you should change your needle size following this simple rule:
* If your knitting is too loose, your gauge (tension) will read that you have less stitches and rows than the given gauge (tension), and you will need to change to a thinner needle to make the stitch size smaller.
* If your knitting is too tight, your gauge (tension) will read that you have more stitches and rows than the given gauge (tension), and you will need to change to a thicker needle to make the stitch size bigger.

Note that if the projects in this book are not knitted to the correct gauge (tension), yarn quantities will be affected.

YARN USED IN THIS BOOK

A selection of yarns from the Rowan Yarn collection have been used to knit all of the designs in this book. Below is a guide to the yarns used.

All Seasons Cotton
Aran-weight cotton and microfiber yarn
60% cotton/40% microfiber
Approximately 98yd (90m) per
1¾oz (50g) ball

Big Wool
Super chunky pure wool
100% merino wool
Approximately 87yd (80m) per
3½oz (100g) ball

Calmer
Soft cotton mix
75% cotton/25% acrylic/microfiber
Approximately 175yd (160m) per
1¾oz (50g) ball

Chunky Print
Chunky pure wool
100% wool
Approximately 109yd (100m) per
3½oz (100g) ball

Cotton Glacé
Lightweight cotton yarn
100% cotton
Approximately 125yd (115m) per
1¾oz (50g) ball

Felted Tweed
Lightweight double knitting
50% merino wool/25% alpaca/25%
viscose
Approximately 191yd (175m) per
1¾oz (50g) ball

Handknit DK Cotton
Medium-weight cotton yarn
100% cotton
Approximately 92yd (85m) per
1¾oz (50g) ball

Kid Classic
Aran weight mohair mix
70% lambswool/26% kid mohair/
4% nylon
Approximately 153yd (140m) per
1¾oz (50g) ball

Kid Silk Haze
Very lightweight mohair yarn
70% super kid mohair/30% silk
Approximately 230yd (210m) per
1 oz (25g) ball

Lurex Shimmer
Very lightweight lurex yarn
80% viscose/20% polyester
Approximately 104yd (95m) per
1oz (25g) ball

Polar
Chunky alpaca mix
60% pure new wool/30% alpaca/
10% acrylic
Approximately 109yd (100m) per
1¾oz (50g) ball

Rowan Denim
Medium-weight cotton yarn
100% cotton
Approximately 101yd (93m) per
1¾oz (50g) ball

Summer Tweed
Aran-weight silk and cotton yarn
70% silk/30% cotton
Approximately 118yd (108m) per
1¾oz (50g) hank

Wool Cotton
Double-knitting-weight wool and
cotton
50% merino wool/50% cotton
Approximately 123yd (113m) per
1¾oz (50g) ball

Yorkshire Tweed DK
Double knitting pure wool
100% pure new wool
Approximately 123yd (113m) per
1¾oz (50g) ball

4-ply Soft
Fine pure wool
100% merino wool
Approximately 191yd (175m) per
1¾oz (50g) ball

ABBREVIATIONS

beg	beginning/begin
cont	continue
cm	centimeter
c4b	cable 4 back: slip next 2 sts onto a cable needle and hold at back of work, k2, then k2 from the cable needle
c4f	cable 4 front: slip next 2 sts onto a cable needle and hold at front of work, k2, then k2 from the cable needle
c6b	cable 6 back: slip next 3 sts onto a cable needle and hold at back of work, k3, then k3 from the cable needle
dec	decrease
g	grams
in	inch
inc	increase
k	knit
k2tog	knit two stitches together.
mb	make bobble: using yarn B, (k1, p1) twice into next st, (turn, p4, turn, k4) twice, turn, p4, turn and sl2, k2tog, psso
mm	millimeter
m1	make one stitch
oz	ounces
p	purl
patt	pattern
pb	place bead: yarn forward, slip bead to front of work, slip 1 st purlwise, take yarn to back of work. Bead will now be sitting in front of slipped stitch
ps	Place sequin: yarn forward, slip sequin to front of work, slip 1 st purlwise, take yarn to back of work. Sequin will now be sitting in front of the slipped stitch
psso	pass slipped stitch over
p2tog	purl two stitches together

rep	repeat
RS	right side of work
sl	slip
st st	stockinette (stocking) stitch
st/sts	stitch/stitches
WS	wrong side of work
yb	yarn back
yf	yarn forward
∗	repeat instructions between ∗ as many times as instructed
( )	repeat instructions between ( ) as many times as instructed.

CONVERSIONS

Needle sizes

US SIZE	METRIC SIZE	OLD UK & CANADIAN SIZE
15	10	000
13	9	00
11	8	0
11	7½	1
10½	7	2
10½	6½	3
10	6	4
9	5½	5
8	5	6
7	4½	7
6	4	8
5	3¾	9
4	3½	–
3	3¼	10
2/3	3	11
2	2¾	12
1	2¼	13
0	2	14

Weights and lengths

oz	=	g × 0.0352
g	=	oz × 28.35
in	=	cm × 0.3937
cm	=	in × 2.54
yd	=	m × 0.9144
m	=	yd × 1.0936

Acknowledgments

Thank you to the following people whose combined talents and skills have come together and helped to make this book possible: Rowan Yarns for allowing me to use their wonderful yarns, and in particular Sharon Brant and Kate Buller for their support and advice; Justina Leitão for her superb styling and design; Neil Sutherland for his fantastic photography; Emma Callery for her excellent editorial skills; Marie Clayton for making the project happen, and Monika Cobel for her perfect knitting. Lastly, thank you to Simon, whose support as always has been unwavering. The publishers would also like to thank Chris and Caroline, Steve and Mhairi for the use of their lovely homes and Homebase (website: www.homebase.co.uk) for the loan of material for photography.

SUPPLIERS

Emma King: www.emmaking.co.uk

Suppliers of Rowan Yarns and Jaeger Handknits

USA
Westminster Fibers, Inc.
4 Townsend West,
Suite 8
Nashua, NH 03063
Tel: 603 886 5041
Fax: 603 886 1056
www.knitrowan.com
E-mail:
knitting@westminsterfibers.com

Canada
Diamond Yarn
9697 St Laurent
Montreal
Quebec H3L 2N1
Tel: 514 388 6188

Diamond Yarn (Toronto)
155 Martin Ross
Unit 3
Toronto
Ontario M3J 2L9
Tel: 416 736 6111

Australia
Rowan at Sunspun
185 Canterbury Road
Canterbury
Victoria 3126
Tel: 03 9830 1609

UK
Rowan Yarns and Jaeger Handknits
Green Lane Mill
Holmfirth
West Yorkshire
HD9 2DX
Tel: 01484 681881
www.knitrowan.com

Suppliers of beads

USA
Global Beads
345 Castro Street
Mountain View, CA 94041
Tel: 650 967 7556
www.globalbeads.com

Keep Me In Stitches
77 Smithtown Boulevard
Smithtown, NY 11787
Tel: 631 724 8111
www.keepmeinstitches1.com

UK
Beadworks (mail order)
16 Redbridge Enterprise Centre
Thompson Close
Ilford
Essex
IG1 1TY
Tel: 020 8553 3240
www.beadworks.co.uk

The Bead Shop
21a Tower Street
Covent Garden
London
WC2H 9NS
Tel: 020 7240 0931

The Brighton Bead Shop (mail order)
21 Sydney Street
Brighton
BN1 4EN
Tel: 01273 675077
Email:
mailbox@beadsunlimited.co.uk
www.beadsunlimited.co.uk

Creative Beadcraft Limited
(mail order)
Denmark Works
Sheepcote Dell Road
Beamond End
Near Amersham
Buckinghamshire
HP7 0RX
Tel: 01494 778818

Ells and Farrier
20 Beak Street
London
W1R 3HA
Tel: 0207 629 9964

Mill Hill Beads
www.millhillbeads.com